Narrated By Mom

The Story of Sultan

Neelam Kashyap

BlueRose ONE.com
Stories Matter
NewDelhi • London

BLUEROSE PUBLISHERS

India | U.K.

BlueRose ONE.com
Stories Matter
NewDelhi • London

For permissions requests or inquiries regarding this publication, please contact:

BLUEROSE PUBLISHERS

www.BlueRoseONE.com
info@bluerosepublishers.com
+91 8882 898 898
+4407342408967

ISBN: 978-93-6261-871-9

Cover design: Muskan Sachdeva

Typesetting: Rohit

First Edition: April 2024

I am highly indebted to our son, Madhav Kashyap. I handed over the manuscript to him, which was in a raw form. He patiently worked hard on it and gave it proper shape of a book. It would not be wrong to say that he has given a body and soul to my book.

I am grateful to Dr. Shivani Shrivastav (Physiotherapist), who volunteered to be the first reader of the manuscript. She gave me insightful feedback saying that it was a unique idea, which pepped up my confidence, encouraged and motivated me to complete the book.

I am also very grateful to Rohit, my book formatter and my niece Kiara Rai, who designed the cover page of this book.

Contents

Chapter 1

My Rescue and Arrival at a New Place

The gentle drizzles of the sky gained momentum and gradually turned into rain that dropped on my sensitive body like hammers. The sky had become ominously dark that evening, with the clouds roaring and thundering as if they would tear the sky apart. The terrible lightning was scary, but at least it gave out some light with its occasional flashes.

I realized that I was lying unconscious on a heap of garbage, with no memory of how I got there. All I remember is that I was in so much pain and stress that I couldn't feel either anymore. Suddenly, I felt the weight of some unknown creature land on me. It had very sharp feet which were almost hurting me. "Its sharp feet will pierce my skin!" I thought. I moved my tail a bit to try and scare it off, then suddenly I felt the caress of soft and loving hands lifting me up. It surprised me when I realized that I was being rescued. The person had a very soft and sweet voice and I think there was another person with them. They seemed to be talking about me. One of them said, "Maybe somebody left it here thinking that it was dead. How awful! That person should have checked whether the puppy is alive or not." They also discussed what they should do with me, whether they should leave me there or take me to their home with them. I had no strength to move but hoped they wouldn't leave me, or I wouldn't make it.

One of them said, "If we leave it here, it will definitely die. I think we should take it with us. At least we will save one helpless puppy." The other girl said, "Garima, my family will never allow an animal to stay in our house, not even for a day. As far as taking him with me goes, the question does not even arise. You have to think about your family." Garima confidently replied, "My family is very open-minded and my parents will be proud to know that I have saved a puppy's life. I will take it home with me. I can't just let him die here like this." After listening to her, the other girl said, "Garima, hearing you say that has relieved me of my guilt. I feel so bad for the poor puppy. My conscience was not allowing me to leave it here and I am cursing the person who left him here on this pile of garbage, they must be very cruel."

The girl named Garima told her friend that today she would go home "by auto" since dogs were not allowed in the metro. She picked me up and wiped down me with her jacket. Once I was fairly dry, she kept me in her bag but kept the cover open. I had a strong feeling that I was in safe and caring hands now. Though I was much drier and lighter, I still felt cold and a little wet. Both the girls walked together for some time, trying to call for an auto.

When one auto came by, Garima sat in it. The driver asked "Where to?"

"Panchkuian Road, Railway Officers' Colony." she gave a brief reply.

When the driver had started the auto and it gained momentum, I felt thrilled. It was as if somebody was gently moving me to and fro. After some time, I was feeling sleepy and very soon even keeping my eyes open felt like an exhausting task. Before I knew it, I was fast asleep.

I woke up when the auto stopped and then Garima got down while holding me carefully. She picked up her bag and asked the auto driver, "How much?"

After making the payment, she walked a little distance and entered a big machine that seemed to go upward. Soon we were at a gate.

Chapter 2

My Survival

After reaching home, she pressed the doorbell. A young boy opened the door, looking thoroughly bored. Garima peeked inside sheepishly, then hid her bag behind her back and crept into the house. She asked the boy to follow her.

Once they were in a room, she opened her bag and showed me to her brother. He was rendered speechless for a moment.

After the brief surprise passed, he hugged me.

"Wow, you brought a puppy home! It's so adorable!" he exclaimed joyfully.

"Thanks! It will stay with us and we can play with it." he continued.

"It will be fun, you know! I always wanted to have a puppy. Thanks again. I love you so much."

When I heard him, a hope arose in my heart that now I would get a home, but soon my hopes were dashed by Garima's reply.

She said, "No, we've to take permission from our parents. Only if they allow us can we keep him." The boy readily agreed and confidently said, "I know our parents well enough to know that they wouldn't say 'no' to such a lovely little puppy."

Her words gave me some solace and I wanted to believe her. She had rekindled my hopes for having and belonging to a home. After a few seconds, Garima gently put me on their bed. In the meantime, one woman entered the room and when she saw me, she asked Garima, "Have you bought another soft toy? Your collection of soft toys is increasing day by day. You're a grownup now, stop this childish habit. Come on, Garima."

Garima had a hearty laugh and said, "No, Mummy, it isn't a soft toy. It's a real puppy. Touch it and see for yourself. It is real!"

Her mother wonderingly touched me and yelled at Garima out of shock. She said, "Why have you brought this sick little puppy home? It looks lifeless, it isn't even moving."

Garima replied, "Mummy, I had also thought that it was dead but I saw that it wagging its tail when a crow was about to peck it. That means it is alive, please give it some milk to drink. It might survive. I have just tried to save its life."

After hearing her out, Garima's mother relented and agreed to feed me with milk. She said, "Children, we don't have a feeding bottle so I will have to feed it with a cotton bud. Garima, go and get some cotton quickly. Madhav, you stay with the puppy and take care of it. I will go to the kitchen and bring some milk for him"

I was very happy to see that an army had readied itself quickly to save my life.

Soon their mother made a cotton bud, warmed some milk, and started feeding me. Both Garima and her brother were anxiously watching me.

The moment I was given some milk, I felt rejuvenated and started dancing with joy. It was not simply milk, but it seemed as if she had given me some life elixir. I could instantly feel the energy that had started flowing through my whole body.

The kids were overjoyed to see me alive. "It's a miracle!" both of them exclaimed. Garima said, "Mom you have done a miracle. You have brought him back to life, even though I was afraid that he might die. You're simply great, I really believe that you have some supernatural powers."

The kids hugged their mother out of joy as they thanked her profusely.

The Mother retorted, "I don't have any supernatural power to save lives. He is alive now because he was already alive. There's no need to say thanks to me, I haven't done anything. I don't have any magical powers to perform any miracles. Understand?"

She said to Garima, "Just take a look at how weak it is. There's no way it will survive. Please leave it outside. The last thing I want is for some animal to die in my household."

I felt extremely sad to listen that I was going to die, and my heart started sinking out of fear. I was just a little puppy who had only lived a few days' life. The very thought of death was gloomy and scary and felt unfair.

Then I gave myself a bit of solace as I thought to myself, "I was in a terrible condition because of hunger but a few drops of milk have given me a new lease on life. If I am regularly given milk, I will definitely live."

This thought gave me the strength to live my life fully.

The Mother insisted that I be dropped at the same place that she had picked me up from. Garima promised that she would definitely do what her mother had asked to do once I had fully recovered. This appeased her mother and she calmed down.

Just then, a man entered the room. He asked Garima, "What is the matter, why do you and Madhav look so sad?"

Garima patiently told him the whole story. "Papa, I was trying to save its life. Have I done something wrong? Have I committed any blunder by helping this puppy?"

Suddenly her papa's anger melted, his facial expressions changed, and he said, "My dear daughter, I am proud of you. You have indeed done a great job. I really appreciate the compassion you have shown to this puppy but you can forget about keeping it with us for life. Now go and sleep."

After this, everybody went to their rooms, and the kids took me to theirs. Madhav brought a bedsheet, prepared a bed for me and then he put me on down on it. Both of them then started talking about me. Madhav said to Garima in a sad tone, "Garima, please do something. I already love this puppy so much. Think of some plan to convince our parents, compel them to change their decision about the puppy."

Garima consoled him and assured him that she would definitely do something. Madhav looked very relaxed when he got her assurance. I wanted to stay awake to listen to what else they said but my stomach was full so I got drowsy and soon I fell asleep.

Chapter 3

I Got a Name

When I woke up the next morning, my fatigue had disappeared completely. I saw that I was in Garima's lap, and she was lovingly caressing me. It made me happy to be in safe and caring hands again. Her brother, Madhav, was also very kind and insisted to Garima that they keep me with them forever.

Garima said, "Madhav, you need to understand that we can't keep him without our parent's consent. We need their permission. I have assured you that I will do something about this, so just have faith in me."

"I know our parents will agree with us. I will have to persuade them myself," Madhav said confidently.

In the meantime, their mother entered the room and started talking to Garima.

"Are both of you awake? Come for breakfast and bring the puppy with you; it's time for his breakfast, too. I'll give him some milk."

She then left the room, and Madhav began talking to Garima.

"Garima, it seems Mumma has a soft spot for him. Soon, I will turn her concern into love for this puppy."

Then they left the room and took me with them for breakfast.

Seeing Madhav's confidence, I became hopeful for a home.

When we reached the dining area, I saw that their mother had kept some milk ready for me. She started feeding me with the bud again and asked somebody to bring breakfast for the family.

She was hardly aware that every drop of milk that she was giving me was filling me with energy. She was feeding me not just with milk but strength, too.

After feeding me, she sat down for breakfast for herself and after finishing it, she asked her domestic helper to get a good feeding bottle for me. When I heard this, I felt very happy. It felt like she was my own mother. Since both the children called their parents Mom and Papa, I, too, decided to call them Mom and Papa.

I had realised that I was recovering quickly and was definitely going to live to a full age. It made me extremely thankful to Garima for saving me, and to mom, for giving me a new lease on life. I was feeling very relieved now, since I was very certain that I was not going to die.

The day passed, and the next morning Madhav brought up the important question of my name to Garima.

"Garima, have you thought about what we should name him?", he asked.

"I have, but I'm not keen on any English names. They're just too common. I'll keep thinking about it, so let me know if you have any unique names in mind."

Madhav said that he could only think of English names. The next day, Garima told Madhav that she now had a name in mind and that if he also liked it, they would finalize it. He excitedly asked her what it was, and then she suggested the name: 'Nawab'.

Madhav anxiously asked her what that meant. She said that it meant 'ruler'. Madhav became very happy with this unique name, and hence 'Nawab' was finalized.

Now I, too, had a name like humans.

A couple of days later, in the morning, I heard Papa yell, "Suku and Manu! Come here and see what I got for you!"

I started wondering who Manu and Suku were... I didn't know that there was one more surprise was awaiting me. Strangely, I saw Garima and Madhav enter the room and reply,

"Yes, Papa? What have you brought for us? Show us!", they said together.

Papa had brought some food for them, which both of them soon got busy eating.

I wondered when their names had been changed, but I couldn't come up with any answers. After many days, I realised that both of them were addressed by two names. It was then that I understood that some human beings have two names, one being their nickname and another name being their formal name.

Now a desire also arose in my heart for Garima to give me a nickname.

Would she give me a nice nickname?

Chapter 4

Reluctant Parents

The next morning, when she was about to leave for her school, Meena asked her who had brought me to them.

"Madam, are you going to keep a pet? It really is a lovely puppy."

She immediately said no.

"Garima found it in a miserable condition, so she has brought it here for now. We aren't going to keep it forever. Once it recovers, we will give it to somebody, but until then both you and Mahinder will have to look after it as well. Both of you should take good care of this puppy until it is in safe hands. Look after it, I have to go to my school now."

Both of them nodded their heads and promised her that they would take good care of me.

I was glad to hear Mummy's caring words. After giving them instructions, she left for her school.

One very shocking development took place the next morning. One of the helpers took me for a walk around twelve o' clock in the afternoon. When we were coming back, I created a bit of a fuss because I wanted him to carry me in his lap. I was too young to walk that far, and moreover, I was not able to see very clearly yet. I thought that my vision was slightly blurred.

Instead of lifting me, he jerked me and slapped me on my head. I was shocked with fear, so I obediently started walking with him.

I was hardly aware that by chance, one kind lady had witnessed all of this from her balcony. After a few minutes, we reached our house.

Suddenly, one of the phones started to ring. I saw Garima pick up the phone. I didn't know who the person on the other side was, but I saw that Garima was shocked to listen to whatever they were saying. She ended the call with a reply.

"Thank you so much, Jasmine Aunty, for telling me this. I will tell this to my mother and she will definitely scold him. How did he dare to slap such a little puppy? Once again thanks, Aunty."

She then put the receiver down and called Madhav, telling him that their helper had struck me. Her voice was shaking in anger. Madhav anxiously asked her how she knew this and who had told her about this, calling their helper cruel.

"Jasmine aunty," she told him. Both of them decided to tell this to their Mom.

When Mom came back from school, they narrated the whole incident to her. She clearly felt very upset and sad to learn that a little puppy had been mistreated by her helper. She spoke to her children in a serious tone.

"Children, now you see what a sad thing it is that this puppy is treated so badly by our helper. It is true that I don't want to keep this puppy for good, but at the same time. I just can't tolerate any cruelty against little Nawab."

Then she lifted me up, kept me on her lap, started caressing me, and continued.

"So don't you think that we should give him to a real dog-loving family, who aren't dependent on their helpers like we are? Do you think we can compel them to love him as you do?"

Both the children promptly replied, "No. We can't compel them... but we can tell this to Papa. They won't dare disobey him! Mom, we desperately want to keep him, and we will ask Papa to scold our helper to make sure this doesn't happen again."

Mom was not at all in a mood to please the children. Besides, Papa was not in favour of keeping me with them forever, either. I had now begun to lose faith in Madhav's confidence and my hope for belonging to a home was also vanishing before me.

When Papa came back home from his office, the kids anxiously reported the slap episode to him. They also requested him to scold that helper. Madhav even emotionally begged him to give them permission to keep me with them forever. I think his anger melted a bit when he saw Madhav requesting this of him with folded hands.

"Children, it is easy to bring a pet home, and it seems easier to take care of it, but it is a big responsibility. I also had a dog when I was a child, and I loved him a lot, but I had to abandon him because he had become a problem for us. Every day, our neighbors used to quarrel with us because the dog used to make their house dirty with his poop. I tried very hard to change his habit to no avail. We were fed up of picking a fight with the neighbour on a daily basis, so we had to make the difficult and tough decision to leave him somewhere else." Papa said to the kids in a sad tone.

"I will definitely scold the helper for slapping this puppy, but do you think that I will be able to change his heart? Do you think every time this happens, your Jasmine aunty will be there to report to you?", he continued.

After this incident, both of the parents had clearly told their children that their demand was unreasonable because everyone was working. Both of them decided that everyone would now start looking for a family that they felt could take proper care of me.

Why did no one ask me what I wanted?

Why did the parents fail to understand that I had become fond of every member of the family and wanted to stay with them forever?

Anyways, I was mentally ready to depart from the family, albeit very reluctantly because I had started loving Garima and Madhav, and they too used to love me a lot. I loved playing with Madhav, and I thought that I would always miss both of them. The love that they had shown me would always be my treasure.

Chapter 5

A Visit to the Veterinary Clinic

A few days later, Mom asked Meena to make my bag ready. Meena anxiously asked her, "Are you giving Nawab to somebody?"

She said, "No. It is true that I want to give him to a family that will take good care of him but he is too weak to be given to somebody right now. We will take him to a veterinary hospital near Tis Hajari Court, which is a government hospital. I want the doctor to give him some tonics or medicine to make him strong." Mom got ready to show me to a doctor to make me physically fit at the earliest and Meena accompanied us. After a somewhat long journey, we reached the veterinary clinic near Tis Hajari court.

When we reached the hospital, Mom got out of the car and Meena picked me up. We went inside and walked past the queue. Mom took me to the doctor and showed me to him. The doctor asked her to wait in the queue, to which she promptly said, "Of course, I will get in the queue, I just want to tell you something first."

The doctor said, "O.K." She said, "When this puppy licks my hands I feel very itchy. Am I allergic to dogs? Is it safe to keep him in our house?"

The doctor coolly replied, "Madam, There's no such disease. Maybe you have never kept a pet so you are worried but I assure you that you are absolutely safe. I think that your problem is only psychological because a dog's saliva never causes any kind of harm or itching."

Mom looked disappointed and went back to join the queue. I had understood that she wanted to get rid of me and she was hoping the doctor would give her an excuse for it. The doctor had declared that her problem was invalid so she looked a bit upset. I was really hurt because Mom was making excuses to get rid of me. Alas!

I saw several dogs and some different kind of animals, who had also come looking for treatment. I also saw a little white puppy with a fractured leg in the hands of a middle aged woman. Mom asked that lady about the fracture in the leg of such a small puppy. She told Mom that her grandson had dropped the puppy accidently and the puppy suffered a fracture in his leg. Mom said in a sad tone, "It's so sad to see such a tiny puppy suffer like this. I hope he gets well soon." Though mom was feeling sorry for the puppy, to me it looked very cute with a small plaster on his small leg. Besides, the colour of the plaster went very well with his white fur. Immediately after thinking it, I regretted having had such a mean thought.

That lady asked Mom how much my family had to pay to buy me. Mom told her the whole incident about how I was brought to their home. After hearing the story, she blessed Mom and said, "You are very lucky to have a black dog without purchasing it or taking it from somebody. God will bless you and your entire family for taking care of this orphaned baby." Mom just smiled and said thanks to her.

That day, I came to know dogs were bought and sold. It was very shocking and unbelievable, and this information was eye-opening for me. Are dogs commodities? Do people purchase them like objects?

We resumed standing in the queue and waiting for our turn. There was a medium-sized animal standing ahead of us. I hadn't seen an animal like that before and wondered what it was.

When she saw it, Mom pointed it out to Meena.

"Look, Meena, this hospital treats goats as well, isn't that nice?"

Meena smiled and nodded his head. I felt very happy that my query was answered and I then discovered a different kind of animal, a 'goat'. I looked around and saw that there were many goats around, who must all have come for treatment.

The goat's diagnosis didn't take much time and soon we were called in by the doctor.

"Next!", he yelled from inside his office.

Mom hurriedly asked Meena to show me to the doctor as she walked in. She told him that I was very weak and that she wanted the doctor to prescribe some good tonics to me. The doctor said that he will definitely would, and then he examined my stomach and eyes.

"Madam, your dog here is too young for tonics, but I can prescribe him a very good food supplement meant specifically for puppies. It will gradually help him overcome his weakness," the doctor said. He wrote something on a piece of paper and said that he had prescribed the supplement on it. Mom took the paper and asked Meena to purchase whatever was written on the paper.

Meena asked the doctor where he could purchase the prescribed medicines, and the doctor gave him the directions to what he called a pharmacy. Meena left for the medical store while we were waiting there, and we stood near the doctor's table.

After a few seconds, it was the little white puppy's turn, the one who had suffered a fracture in his leg. When the doctor had examined the puppy, her owner started narrating my story to the doctor about how I was rescued by Garima and how my family was taking care of me. The doctor was listening to the lady very attentively, and I felt like he was taking interest in my story. He looked very impressed with my family and said thanked mom for saving the life of a puppy.

When the lady was through, the doctor told Mom that she was very lucky to have a black dog that she had neither bought nor was gifted. He said that getting a black dog was a good omen and that I was a godsend for her, telling her that I was a purebred Labrador.

Mom was surprised to hear that. She asked him whether he really believed in what he had said, to which the doctor said, "Yes, I do. You must think how I can believe in superstitions despite being a doctor. Madam, it is my strong belief because I have seen families getting benefitted by having a black dog."

I felt very lucky and proud when I heard that I was a good omen. This is how I came to know that I was 'black', though just like my name, I didn't know the meaning of the word.

Wasn't it funny to have two identities without knowing their meanings? I also didn't know the meaning of omen, but I knew one thing for sure: if the word good is attached with any other word, it is appreciation, because when I do something they like, my family members often say the word "good" to me and show their love to me afterwards.

Chapter 6

Amar Singh Treated Me

Two-three days later, in the morning, a man came to our house holding a file in his hands. Papa took the file and started reading it. After reading the papers, he took a pen and wrote something on them. The man was about to leave after this, but Papa asked him to wait for some time. He then asked Meena to bring some tea and snacks for him. Meena went towards the kitchen and Papa asked the man to have a seat as he started talking to the man.

"Amar Singh, you have a lot of knowledge about dogs. My daughter has brought me a little puppy. I want you to examine it and tell us what you see."

"I'll be sure to guide you with whatever little knowledge I have. Where is the puppy?", Amar Singh asked in a curious tone.

Papa picked me up from one side of the sofa and kept me on the table in front of both of them. Amar Singh exclaimed, "Sir, I have never seen such a quiet dog before. It was sitting here all this time but I was not able to sense his presence." He continued, "Sir, I have also never seen a dog with such a dark black colour. His colour and coat are amazing!"

By that time, Mom had also come to the living room and taken a seat. Amar Singh then took me on his lap and examined me thoroughly.

He said that my eyes had not fully opened yet. I think that he was a keen observer because he also spotted a mark on my tail and talked about it in detail.

"A mother dog cleans her puppies by licking them. I think his mother probably didn't clean him here, that must be why he does not have any hair on this spot."

Mom looked very sad to hear this. "Is it a major problem? Will his tail ever become normal? Should I take him to some hospital?", she asked so many questions, worryingly.

He confidently replied to reassure her. "Madam, you don't need to worry at all. I will make an ointment for him. You just have to ensure that it is applied regularly every day on his tail. I promise you that he will be alright."

He then examined my eyes and told her that according to his observation, I was severely weak and anaemic, maybe because of starvation.

When Mom heard this, her anxious tone returned.

"Can we give him something to help him recover from this weakness? I had taken him to the Tis Hazari clinic, but the doctor said that it is too early to give some tonics to him."

Amar Singh also confirmed it, he advised Mom to should wait for around two months. By the time he said this, snacks were served to him.

Once again, he assured the parents that he would cure the spot on my tail. He returned the next day and brought some ointment with him. After mixing it with some oil, he applied it to my tail. Afterwards, he called Mahinder and taught him how to mix the ointment and how much should be applied on the spot on my tail.

Mahinder then started applying the ointment to my tail every day, and he did so very religiously. Because it was my tail, I couldn't see whether there was any improvement or not but I had faith in Mahinder's efforts. Many days later, Amar Singh returned to our house to check on my tail. He looked very happy and satisfied after taking a look at it again. He then asked Mom to examine for herself and she exclaimed, "Wow, it's like magic! He has started growing hair again. How can I thank you?"

Amar Singh politely said that he was happy to see that the spot had disappeared with his ointment and didn't want anything else.

When I heard this, I, too, was relieved to get rid of the bald spot on my tail.

Chapter 7

A Farewell Video

One day, Papa asked Amar Singh to visit our house, saying that he had something serious on his mind. Once he had arrived, Papa asked him to take a seat and then asked Meena to bring some snacks for him. Papa then asked Mom to come to the living room.

While sipping his tea, Amar Singh asked Papa why he had been called and if there was anything wrong with me.

"He is alright. Actually, I have called you to tell you that we are not interested in keeping Nawab. All of us are working, so there's no one who will take care of him. I wanted to ask you to find a dog-loving family for him. After all, dogs require a lot of attention and care, which we can't always provide for him".

Amar Singh, to my surprise, tried to convince the parents to change their mind.

"Sir, you have a lot of manpower at home. You have Mahinder and Meena, and they will take care of him. If anything happens to him then I am always at your service. I will come from time to time to see if he faces any problems. It is a good omen to keep a black dog and the best part is that you have neither bought him nor got him as a gift. You are fortunate that he has come to your family on his own, right from the beginning. I used to think that your family needed a dog and God has given you not just any dog but a pure black dog. Sir, believe me, he is a Godsend for you."

This was enough to trigger mom's anger. She looked irritated with that argument and said to him, "Amar Singh, kids are raised by the parents themselves, we can not hand over this responsibility to someone else. If this puppy stays here he will be raised like our own child, or he won't stay here at all. Besides, I don't believe in superstitions like black dogs being a good omen. Our deeds decide our fate, not a dog. The doctor also said the same thing and I am surprised that even in the 21st century we believe in these things. Ridiculous!"

Amar Singh couldn't utter a single word after listening to this weird argument. He politely said, "Sir, I will try my best to find a very good family for him but please give me some time." Papa said, "Please try to do this at the earliest because my children are getting fond of him and I want to give him to a family before it is too late and they get too attached. Neither my wife nor I want to keep him as a pet so please do it as soon as possible."

I was also surprised over the argument that a dog could be raised like one's own child,. After all, a dog is dog and he is raised like a dog, not like a human. I thought, "There is no need to make me their own child, I am happy to live like a pet."

Several days later, Amar Singh returned to our house. After being greeted well by both the parents., he said to Papa, "Sir, you had asked me to find a suitable family for Nawab and now I have found one. They are looking for a Labrador puppy and they were very happy to know that Nawab is jet black, they want to come to your house to see him. They want to get a puppy soon because their own Labrador dog has died recently."

"Sir, I think that this is perfect family for Nawab, but they are very particular about the health of the puppy. I think that Nawab is very weak right now so you have to make him healthy first. They will visit your house to see Nawab, maybe next week." he continued.

Both the parents looked very happy. Papa said to Amar Singh, "I am very happy to know that you have really obliged us for giving Nawab to a loving family. Madam will look after Nawab well, she will leave no stone unturned in making him healthy."

I felt very sad to listen to this news, even though I was mentally ready for this. I used to remind myself daily that I would have to leave this family but one thing that I didn't like was the attitude of both the parents. On one hand, they wanted to get rid of me. On the other hand, they had been showing me their love and were taking very good care of me, right from the beginning.

I couldn't help but feel sad because the very thought of leaving this caring and loving family was scary. Both the kids were also sad because now they were emotionally attached with me, as I was with them. Only the parents looked relieved with the thought of sending me away to some other place.

Was I a burden on them? Were they really this desperate to be rid of me?

Initially, both Garima and Madhav opposed this decision, but later on they compromised on giving me to some other family. Or rather, it would be more appropriate to say that they had no other option but to surrender.

The morning after, Garima and Madhav told me that they wanted to make a video of me, which made me feel very special. They started making a video in which I was jumping and running around them enthusiastically. I was happy that I was important enough for them to film me, so I ran faster and jumped higher and higher, just to make them happy.

While taking the video, Garima told me, "Nawab, this is your farewell video. Tomorrow you will join a new family... whenever we miss you, we'll watch your video. I wish our family would have kept you with us but we've to obey our parents. We're sorry for being so helpless.... just remember that we've enjoyed every moment that we've spent with you."

Hearing this felt like being dropped from the sky. I immediately stopped jumping and running feeling like a fool for dancing at my own farewell. "It's a time for weeping and here I am jumping and dancing. Why did I ever become emotionally attached to Garima and Madhav? Was that a mistake?", I thought.

My heart started sinking and I started to feel numb. When Madhav saw that I had stopped jumping, he said to Garima, "Maybe he's tired of this hectic exercise. Let's not make him any more tired; let him sit down and take some rest." They picked me up and sat me down on the sofa. Both of them then started kissing and patting me.

They also clicked a few photographs with me. I wanted to tell them, "Please stop giving me so much love, it will make it far too difficult to forget you. My life will become very miserable without the both of you, so please, leave me alone." I tried to tell them, in my own language but they couldn't understand and kept showering their love on me, unaware of my pain. Their parents also came into the room and joined in but I couldn't appreciate their love. Garima then took me on her lap and started caressing me as I laid there, motionless. When did I fall asleep? I can't remember.

Chapter 8

I Faced a Rejection

I was feeling very anxious the following day. Madhav was caressing me as I was sitting still in Garima's lap. Suddenly, the doorbell rang, but I didn't budge unlike usual. Mahinder went ahead and opened the door. As anticipated, two strangers and Amar Singh were standing right outside. Mahinder called them in and asked them to take their seats, Amar Singh asked him to call our parents. He went inside and called both of them, telling them to come into the living room. Papa welcomed them and asked them if they would prefer tea or coffee. One of the strangers politely refused and said, "I am sorry, we are in a hurry. I have to go somewhere, so kindly just show us the puppy."

I had understood very well that they have come to take me with them so I did not welcome them. Rather, I was annoyed with papa for giving them such a warm welcome. I had no desire to entertain them, instead, I wanted to chase them away. If only I could!

I heard the strangers and Amar Singh talking to each other, that is how I came to know that they were father and son. One of them said to our papa, "We had a Labrador whom we loved a lot. He had grown old and has recently died. Since we are missing our dog, we want his replacement. We want to fill that void in our life with another dog." Papa said, "I can understand your feelings, you seem to be fond of dogs.

Actually, we always wanted to give him to a loving family, one that can give him love and care that he deserves."

I thought about the stranger. "I can't appreciate your feelings", I felt. "You want an alternative or a replacement for your loving dog. Is that all I will be to you? A replacement? Can a dog ever replace another one? No! Every dog has his own personality and identity. I also have an identity and personality of my own just like you human beings do. After all, I am the Nawab (ruler) of this family.

Amar Singh picked me up and showed me to the father-son duo. The father took me on his lap and started seeing me. Or rather, inspecting me. He turned me upside-down and left to right. I thought, "Why are you humiliating me? You're tossing me and turning me as if I am no more than a stone. I have feelings just like human beings, stupid!" He widened my eyelids to check my eyes and then he inspected my tail. He whispered in Amar Singh's ear, "This puppy is very weak and anaemic and I don't think that he will survive and live for much longer. We don't want this weakling." After this, father and son exchanged glances, then looked at me and started making faces. I was watching them keenly. Though the stranger had said those words to Amar Singh in whispers, I had heard him clearly.

Once I knew that they were not going to adopt me, I felt very happy. However, I got very angry at the way they were inspecting me. I was not lifeless, I was a living being. I couldn't help but feel terrible about the way they were making faces at me. If they didn't like me they, could have simply said no! There was no need to humiliate me by inspecting me up and down like an object.

Soon, the strangers declared that they were not interested in me and they rejected me by calling me sick and weak.

I felt very happy at their rejection, thinking that now I wouldn't have to go to some stranger's family and would get to stay here, forever. After some time, they finally went away and I was overjoyed, as were the kids.

Though I was relieved, I asked myself, "Was our happiness going to last forever?"

Chapter 9

Healthy Nawab

After the rejection, Mom took it as a challenge to make me healthier. She started following the diet chart regularly; I think she took this rejection a personal insult. How could I convey to her that they had not insulted her at all but rather me? They were making dirty faces at me; treating me as if I were trash or some filthy thing. I just wasn't able to convey it to her because she didn't understand my signs or my language. If there was somebody who should have felt bad about those strangers' attitude, it was definitely me, not Mom. I also wondered how they were so sure that I was a weakling and was definitely not going to survive. Did they have some supernatural powers with which they had predicted this?

Two three days later, Mom spoke to Mahinder about me, "We are particular about his diet but I think we've to make him internally strong. Should I give him a massage with oil just like we massage human babies?" Mahinder immediately said, "Madam, human babies are given a bath after the massage. We can't give him a bath every day. Amar Singh has told us to bathe him twice a month. If we can't bathe him daily, the oil will gather dust on him after every walk and he might get some skin disease from it." Mom seemed fully convinced and said, "You're absolutely right. I think we should think of giving him some physical exercise instead. Do you have anything in mind?" Mahinder said that he was clueless. Mom then asked Meena but he also said the same thing. A few days later, Mom asked Mahinder to carry me to our colony's park. She asked him to stand away from her a little and handed over me to him. Then she asked him to put me on the ground. The moment he kept me down, I instinctively ran towards Mom. She then took me on her lap and handed me back over to Mahinder. They did this over and over again several more times. Once they could tell I was slowing down, they brought me back home. This routine continued for about two months. I could really feel the difference, it felt like my legs were becoming stronger.

By now I was very confused about the parents' attitudes. I couldn't decide whether they loved me or not. On the one hand, they used to clean my pee and potty, which I used to do here and there. I also used to make heaps of potty in the balcony at night and I would see mom cleaning it in the morning, almost like a ritual, without ever frowning. I had never seen her making a dirty face, so I had assumed that they loved me. Sometimes papa also used to clean my poop and neither of them ever asked their helpers to clean it. Right from my first day in this family, mom had always taken care of my health and needs. She had never been rude to me, which led me to believe that they loved me a lot. On the other hand, they wanted to give me away to some other family like I was just some object they could pass around, like I had no feelings about my life being changed like this. Their mixed signals meant that I couldn't make up my mind about how they truly felt about me.

Why they were not expressing their love for me? Gradually, I started realising that they had developed a soft spot for me but weren't ready to accept this. I was very confident that sooner or later, they would willingly accept me.

I was sure that they would gladly accept me...

Wouldn't they?

Chapter 10

I Went Missing

One day, it just so happened that Mom, Garima and Madhav were at home during the daytime. Perhaps it was their holiday? Every member of the family was busy with their work. There was too much commotion in the living room because Mahinder and Meena were cleaning the room with a vacuum cleaner. Such a loud noise was unbearable for me, besides, I was feeling very sleepy after having had my breakfast. I started looking out for a quiet place to take a hassle-free nap, so I toured the entire house to find the perfect spot, and I finally found a table in the corner in one of the bedrooms. The table had two surfaces, one was the top which people had put a lot of things on, and one was just above the ground, empty and more comfortable than the cold floor.

"Wow, this spot will be perfect for sleeping on, no one will disturb me here. I can get some sound sleep here," I thought. I congratulated myself for finding an isolated and quiet place, and I quickly jumped and fell asleep on the part of the table that was just above the ground.

I woke up suddenly when I heard a loud cry mixed with happiness and surprise. It was Meena!

"Look, he's here! He's here, I found him. Madam, he is here!" he exclaimed loudly.

All the family members came running to that room and surrounded me. Mom immediately picked me up, hugged me tightly, and heaved a sigh of relief. To my surprise, she suddenly started kissing me vehemently. Why were all the family members now all around me? I had no idea what was happening, and I couldn't guess what the matter was.

Meena started laughing and said, "Madam, there we were, so worried about him, and here he's sleeping soundly, unaware of our concern."

Garima nodded and added, "We were looking for you everywhere in the house!" We were all looking for you like crazy. We looked under the mattresses, the sofa, and even the almirahs for you."

She continued, "When we couldn't find you indoors, we went to the balcony, but we couldn't find you there, either," she said. "We were getting anxious about you until mom finally decided that you had drowned in the toilet in the bathroom, which has an Indian seat. We were all on the verge of tears." Garima further said that Mummy was very upset and worried at the thought of me having gone missing. It made me feel sorry for her anxiety, but it also made me happy to know that she loved me enough to miss me if I was gone.

I was reassured that mom definitely loved me a lot. This thought made me so happy! After this incident, Mom tied a ribbon with a ghungroo (small ringing bell) around my neck, so that they could hear the bell and know where I was.

This really was an unforgettable incident.

Chapter 11

A War of Wits

I can recall that Mom used to take me to the balcony to give me toilet training. I remember that she used to sing, "Su–su maaiyan, mere kallu ne paiyan." (My lovely Blackey is peeing.) I used to proudly pee as if I was doing a great job because I enjoyed Mummy's rhymes. After I was done, she would happily bring me back inside.

Mom wanted to give me some toilet training because I used to pee just about anywhere in the house. She didn't know how to go about doing that, so she asked Garima for help.

Garima told her that she would look for a solution on the "internet". After looking at her phone for some time, she talked to Mummy about her ideas.

"There's something available online that you can use. It's called 'Good Puppy Spray'. You spray it where you want him to go, and then you bring him near it. It'll train him to use that spot in the future. I'll order some."

When the product reached us, Mom asked Mahinder to use it in the bathroom and start my toilet training. When he took me there, to my disgust, the spray smelled terrible! It smelled just like urine, and I ran out of the room the moment he put me down. Mahinder brought this to Mom's attention. She politely told him to have patience and keep trying to use it for some more days, saying that it might take me time to develop a habit and that it was needed to make sure I wasn't making the house dirty.

After a few days, Mahinder told Mom that the spray wasn't working and that he should maybe increase how much spray he actually uses, to which Mom agreed. He did as he was instructed, and before I knew it, the entire house smelled terrible! I ran out of the bathroom he had put me in, but the smell wouldn't leave me no matter what room I tried to escape into.

"Mahinder, did you spray the whole bottle all at once?", Mom shouted from another room. "Open all the doors and windows!", she yelled again, sounding like she was pinching her nose shut.

Since the smell had spread throughout the entire house, all the windows were opened to let the smell waft out. Once we got some relief from the smell, we were able to breathe comfortably again. I thought that after this incident, Mahinder would stop his routine exercise with the spray. I was surprised, then, because Mahinder proved to be very stubborn and used the spray again the very next day. Then he took me to the bathroom, and the moment he kept me down, I immediately ran out. If he was going to be so stubborn about this, I was going to be even more stubborn than him.

He kept up the practice for several days. He would pick me up and take me to the bathroom. The moment he would keep me down, I would run out. This routine kept going on and on for several days, without yielding any result. I was determined to not give up so easily. For me, it was a self-declared war between myself and Mahinder. I was playing my role very patiently, but it seemed that Mahinder was losing his patience. He continued with his practice for two more days, although half-heartedly. The next day, he requested Mom to let him discontinue this daily exercise, and to my surprise Mom readily agreed.

Yes! I had won!

After this incident, the idea was dropped and Good Puppy Spray was kept on the balcony for good.

Chapter 12

My Second Farewell

After several days, Inspector Amar Singh came to our house again, but this time he came empty-handed. Why was there no paper or file in his hands?

"What bad news have you brought with you this time? How will you break my heart now?", I wondered.

My apprehension was right, as he had definitely brought bad news for me. I understood that my days were numbered here and I was mentally prepared to listen to something terrible from him, to which he delivered.

He was given a warm welcome by the parents, and he immediately began talking.

"Sir, I have found a loving family for Nawab. They are my relatives and their children are crazy for a dog. They live in a village in Gurgaon, and they don't even care to inspect Nawab. They want him as he is."

When I heard this, I felt like throwing stones at him. There were none in the house at that time, so I wanted to fling the snacks that he was devouring at my expense.

I had to bear more farewell trauma. One more video was made, but this time I neither danced nor jumped because my heart was sinking. I felt like both the parents had been very cruel to me. It seemed like they never considered that this separation could be disastrous for me. I wondered why the parents wanted to send me somewhere else, even though I had now stopped peeing or pooping in the house. I had never damaged any furniture or anything else, so why?

Amar Singh told Papa that he would come to get me on Saturday, and to keep a bag of my belongings ready. Both the parents expressed their gratitude to him, after which he went back home. The parents announced to the whole family that I, Nawab, would join a new family on Saturday. Garima and Madhav were desperately requesting the parents to keep me with them forever, but they didn't budge at all. I was really very, very sad!

Amar Singh came on the assigned date, had a seat, and enjoyed a feast. In the meantime, my bag was packed and all the family members started showering their love on me. Both the parents kissed me and wished me good luck, but there was no way I could appreciate their love and their wishes. After some time, Amar Singh picked me up and took me with him along with my baggage.

He came downstairs and put me in my bag, leaving some space open so that I could breathe, and then he hung the bag around his shoulder and started his bike. Suddenly, his mobile phone rang and he stopped driving the bike. I tried to listen in but had no idea what kind of conversation was taking place. Amar Singh said O.K. a few times and started waiting in the shade. I had no idea what the matter was but a hope arose in my heart. Maybe my family wanted me back!? Alas! It was a false hope.

I saw Mom's car come near us and stop. The driver opened the door for us. Amar Singh entered the car, brought me out of the bag, and kept me on his lap. As the driver started the car, I tried to turn around to see the colony where I had spent some unforgettable days of my life. I looked back to see the balcony where I used to proudly pee while Mom would sing me rhymes.

I was so disheartened that I was in a state of complete hopelessness. Just then, a sense of self-respect arose in my heart and I decided that I would never join this family again. They were ruthlessly sending me away, so I would never come to this family again. Even if they called me back themselves. Never, ever!

The thought of being proud was satisfying and my agitated mind became somewhat calm.

Soon we had crossed Connaught Place and came out on a road which I had never seen before. Amar Singh spoke to the driver.

"This road goes straight to Gurgaon, don't take any turns. Keep driving straight."

I had lots of apprehensions about my "new family". I missed Madhav and Garima and the parents too, but now I wanted to erase those sweet memories forever. Perhaps it was in my own interest to forget about my previous family and adopt the new family wholeheartedly.

Chapter 13

My New Family

Finally, we reached our destination. Amar Singh took me to a village-like place. When we arrived, I was shocked to see that it was a crowded house full of half-naked children!

All the children surrounded me because they were very happy and over-excited to have a puppy. Soon, news of my arrival spread in the neighborhood and some more children came to see me. I was treated like a V.I.P., but my fame didn't lessen my pain. The children of the house were proudly showing me off to the others, who congratulated them and asked and begged Amar Singh to get each of them a puppy, too.

One child asked Amar Singh what my name was. "His name is Nawab. You can call him that, or if you don't like it, you can give him a new name".

The children said that they liked my name and that they wouldn't change it. One child asked him when he would get his family a puppy of their own.

He promised him that if he found another puppy like me, he would definitely give it to him. I, meanwhile, was feeling mixed feelings of happiness and sadness. Perhaps I was happy to see the joyous faces of the children, but at the same time, I felt sad over my separation. I couldn't understand what kind of dog lover Amar Singh was... he boasted of spending his entire life with dogs, and yet, he couldn't even understand the pain of one little dog.

"Does he think only people have feelings?", I thought to myself. "Does my last family think that animals can be sent anywhere, anytime? Are we supposed to be treated like rocks, like we have no feelings? Don't we also get emotionally attached to our families? How can Amar Singh just take me from one place to another like some lifeless object?"

I soon realized that I had to stop thinking like this because if it weren't for him, I probably would have been given away to some unknown person. At least these people were Amar Singh's relatives and he was sure that this family wouldn't insult me by inspecting me and would accept me as I was.

Now I no longer held any grudges against him. If someone was to be blamed, then surely it was the parents in that family. Why did they wait for three months? Why did they not leave me on the same street where Garima had found me? Why did they shower so much love on me? I wished that Garima hadn't picked me up and she had just let me die there. At least I would have died without any painful memories. Now, I had sweet and unforgettable memories of my previous family which wouldn't let me live peacefully with the loving kids in my new home-to-be.

When I came out of my thoughts, I heard Amar Singh explaining to the family how to take care of a puppy dog and what they should and shouldn't do with a dog. The family served him some tea and snacks and later he was served lunch. They also gave me some milk to drink.

The neighbourhood children played with me with a ball but now even chasing and playing with a ball couldn't bring me joy. After an hour or so, Amar Singh left. The neighbourhood kids followed him out of the house after making the promise that they would come back soon to play with me. The children used to offer me biscuits whenever they would see me, but eating biscuits did nothing to please me. I used to eat those biscuits reluctantly, just to satisfy them because I didn't want to break their hearts.

It was very hot in this house because they didn't have an A.C. anywhere. They had a big machine which made a loud noise but gave out somewhat cool air. These children were very rustic in their manners. I couldn't understand why they were half-dressed. The youngest child, around three years of age, was roaming around fully naked like me and other animals. At first, I had thought that he was also from the animal kingdom, but soon I realised that he was a human child because he was walking on his two feet unlike us. He came near me and asked me to play with him, but I didn't show any interest. He stood there for a few seconds, then went away.

I realised that my dream of maintaining my self-respect and dignity was crumbling before me. I wasn't able to control my emotions and soon I had dropped the dream of maintaining self-respect. Once again, I had a longing to join my original family. I was praying very hard to go back to them.

For the first time, I cried about my being a helpless animal. I couldn't understand the language that my supposed new family members were speaking. My first family used to speak in English which I had also started.

To understand. I could also follow Hindi because the family used this language with their domestic helpers.

Everyone was so polished there, so well behaved and soft-spoken, unlike this family where all the members almost used to yell at each other. I had spent an afternoon, evening and one night there and I felt like time was passing very slowly.

I wanted to run back to them, but I was unsure whether my previous family would keep me or not. Not wanting to be reunited only to be separated again, I dropped the idea of running away and started mentally preparing myself to stay here forever. I realized that I had to start adjusting myself to my new surroundings.

It was best that I accept this new family wholeheartedly, and start living in the present instead of past.

Chapter 14

An Emotional Reunion

The next day, in the morning, I was surprised to see Pawan and Meena at the door. I was so happy to see known faces that a thought instantly came to my mind:

"Maybe they've come to take me back!"

My heart started beating fast but I soon controlled my emotions because I didn't want to keep up any false hopes. Then I thought they must have come to know about my well-being or to hand over my leftover belongings to this family. I was surprised to hear that they were seeking apologies from my new family. After some time, Meena took out his mobile phone, dialled a number, and said, "Madam, these people are not agreeing and their eldest daughter wants to talk to you, so please talk to her."

Then he handed over the phone to the girl and the dialogue between this 'madam' and the girl continued for quite some time. The girl was giving several reasonings like, "Madam, did we ask you to give us your puppy? Is this a prank that you are playing with us?" She kept arguing with whoever she was talking to. The conversation continued for some time. Finally, the girl seemed to accept something the other person had said.

"Fine, I will pack his bag, but you should know that this is just not fair. First, you give us your puppy willingly, and now you want him back? Madam, this is just cruel."

I don't know what the madam said from the other side, but I could make out from the girl's facial expressions that she looked defeated and soon, she surrendered.

She asked Meena and Pawan to sit and asked them for tea or something cold, but both of them politely refused to have anything. She also asked them to wait for some time and entered a room. The whole situation had made me confused because I couldn't make out what was going on. My senses had become very numb and couldn't feel anything. I was sitting like a silent spectator and watching everything motionlessly.

I noticed that a complete silence had spread in the house. All the children were sitting quietly with sad looks on their faces. Even the elders of the family were looking sad, which only increased my confusion. What was happening?

Suddenly, the girl came out with my packed bag and gave it to Meena. He held the bag and picked me up, and soon the mystery was solved to me. I was going back! I felt a happiness I couldn't describe. I also felt sorry for the children who were looking very sad like the other members of the family, but for now, my joy knew no bounds. I had never imagined that I would ever get an opportunity to go back to my original home and meet Garima and Madhav again.

The children requested Meena to let me stay there for some more time, but Meena had now become more assertive.

"Look. We understand your feelings, but we are helpless. We have to do as our madam says. Besides, we've come here from far away. We have a lot of distance to cover and madam is not feeling well in his absence. Now, please excuse us."

The children seemed to understand that there was now no point in arguing with Meena, so they said their goodbyes to me with heavy hearts. I also bid them farewell but at the same time, I was getting impatient to go back.

Both Pawan and Meena came out of the house and sat on a motorbike. Pawan took the driver's seat and kept my bag with him, while Meena took the back seat and adjusted me well on his lap as he held me tightly.

"Are you alright?", he asked me. "We have come to take you back. I had never imagined that madam would love you so much. You will soon be with your real family. Happy?"

Pawan asked Meena if he was ready, and started the bike as soon as Meena said yes.

I heard a kick and the bike roared to life, and we started on a known journey. A journey to my house, a journey for my reunion! My heartbeat skyrocketed out of excitement and happiness. I was lost in daydreams, when suddenly Pawan stopped the bike. For a moment, my mind froze out of fear. I thought for a second that he would reverse the bike, and take me back to that family again. That all of this was just some cruel joke being played on me.

Soon I realised that he had just stopped for a red signal. The bike started again when the signal turned green. Now I was assured that we were finally going back to my real and original family.

It took us a lot of time to reach our colony. We reached the same building and entered the lift. At last, the third floor came and we reached the door of the house. My heart started beating very fast. Meena pressed the doorbell. To my joy, mom opened the door!

There were tears in her eyes and in mine, too. The moment she saw me, she took me in her hands and started kissing me vehemently, saying sorry again and again. I could feel motherly warmth in her touch. I felt as if I was entering her heart and she was entering mine. When I raised my head, I saw that the entire family was there to receive me.

Both Garima and Madhav looked happier than ever. I was relieved that I was back and I had realised that I had joined my family, where I actually belonged.

My joy couldn't be expressed in words. I was so happy to be with Garima and Madhav again!

This reunion made both Pawan and Meena very emotional. Everyone was speechless. No one had any words to express their feelings, so our eyes became our means of communication. Our eyes were speaking volumes when words were failing us.

Finally, Pawan broke the silence and said to Mom, "Madam, please don't give him away to anybody again. Look at your condition and his, too. Both of you look miserable. I have always seen Nawab as playful, but today I saw him sitting quietly in a corner with a sad look on his face as if he had been exiled. I have always seen him being happy and lively in your house."

"I had committed a big blunder, and I now promise before all of you that I will never repeat it", Mom said. "I want to seek an apology from everyone here, especially Nawab. I don't know how the thought of sending him away lingered for so long in my stupid mind. I can't change the past, but I will gladly correct my mistake." Papa intervened and said, "Forget about all that. All's well that ends well."

Everyone looked very emotional and happy. As for me, my joy knew no bounds!

Chapter 15

The Pain of Separation

Madhav and Garima were too excited to see me again, as was I. Now I truly felt like I was very precious to the entire family. Mom and Papa took me with them on the sofa and started caressing me. I think they wanted to shower all the love on me which they had been hiding from me all this time.

Though I was reunited with the family, it took me a long time to forget the pain of separation. The fear of being separated again had crept into my mind and heart. I would often have nightmares that I had been abandoned in a lonely place, where there was no one to look after me. I used to get very scared but when I would get up, I would find myself among my family. Waking up to being around my family was a relief, but the nightmares were really scary. I wanted to bring an end to them, an end to this fear.

I couldn't understand why I had been sent away to a new place, then called back the very next day. Maybe I had unknowingly done something bad for which I was punished? I hadn't hurt anyone. I hadn't barked at anyone unnecessarily. I thought I hadn't scratched any furniture or anything, but as I was going through my memories, I remembered that I had once chewed up Garima's slippers. Was that my mistake? It had happened long ago, could it really have been the reason I was sent away?.

While I was thinking about this, I heard Mom, Garima and Papa were arguing over something. I immediately ran into the room they were in to know what the matter was. I heard Papa and Garima talking to mummy. They were asking her to leave her job and take care of me full-time. She sounded shocked, asking them if they were joking. Both of them told her that they were serious.

Mom said that she couldn't believe what they were saying. "Firstly, I can't believe that both of you are serious. If at all you are serious, I don't know whether to laugh or cry over your idea. You're both so invested in Sultan that you have no idea what you're actually saying."

I felt the same. After all, I already had two helpers who took very good care of me in her absence. Mummy quitting her job just seemed like a very unnecessary sacrifice. Why should she have to resign?

Mummy just gave both Papa and Garima a straight-out "No." as a response, and my worries vanished. Papa and Garima looked disappointed, but I was relieved and thankful to Mom that she said that. Besides, Jasmine aunty also had a job as a doctor, but she still took care of her Gabbar, so why should Mom have to leave hers?

Nobody in this family was leaving any stone unturned in taking good care of me, so I didn't feel like anyone else needed to stop everything else to take care of me as Papa and Garima wanted. The idea of leaving her job seemed silly.

Now I was assured that this was my permanent family and I was going to live there forever. I was very angry with my family for trying to give me to other people, but now I wanted to forget the whole separation episode altogether. Today our family consisted of five members including me. A small and happy family indeed!

Chapter 16

I Got a New Name

After a few days, Mom called all the family members in the living room. Mahinder and Meena were also asked to gather there, and I was already present. Garima asked Mom why she had called all of them there, and if there was some serious problem.

"Have some patience," she replied to Garima. "I called everyone here to make a very important announcement about him," she said as she pointed towards me. Madhav immediately lost his patience upon hearing this, and spoke in an agitated tone.

"Don't tell me you're planning to give him away to someone again! If you are, give me to them, too. I'm going wherever he's going!"

He looked upset and it scared me, too. "At least I would have Madhav with me this time, if not Garima", I thought to myself. But what kind of parents would send their own child away?

Mom smilingly reassured both Madhav and I. "No one is going anywhere, Madhav. Please don't jump to conclusions so hastily. I have called everyone here to tell all of you that I have decided to give Nawab a new name. Any guesses?"

"Bruno!", someone yelled. "Sheru!", another proposed.

"Rocky" was another guess.

"Those are all very old-fashioned names, and I don't think they suit his personality. I have thought of one that does. How about Sultan? His name will mean 'sovereign king', and his nickname will be 'Sallu'. How's that?"

Everyone started clapping when they heard both of those names. I was overjoyed to have to now have a name that sounded so grand, and a nickname to go along with it, just like Garima and Madhav had. Garima picked me up and congratulated me, saying that my name went perfectly with my personality.

"Maybe the name I gave you wasn't that good", Garima thought out loud. "I'll call you by your nickname. Sallu!"

Everyone congratulated me, and I felt very special.

After mom's announcement, Madhav felt guilty and apologized to Mom. "I'm really sorry, Mummy. I misunderstood you and jumped to conclusions. You've given him a very unique and suitable name. I wanted to ask you, though… what state is he the Sultan of?"

"Of our sweet home," Mom replied. Papa then picked me up and hugged me, telling me that from today, I was the emperor of this household. My joy knew no bounds! I felt like I was on cloud nine. Me! The emperor!

Now Mom had made a little change in her rhyming, while taking me to the balcony for my toilet training, "Su-Su maiyan, mere Sallu ne paiyan." (My little, sweet, Sultan is peeing.) I used to proudly pee enjoying the rhyme. I liked this rhyming more than the previous one because it mentioned my nickname, too.

It felt great to me to now have a nickname of my own, just like Suku and Manu.

Chapter 17

My GPS

One day, Mom's brother came over to see me. He saw me wearing a small bell tied around my neck with a ribbon, and he didn't sound very pleased to see it.

"Didi, why have you tied a *ghungroo* (small ringing bell) around a male dog's neck? That's so embarrassing. Don't make him dress like a girl."

Maybe he was right, but I knew that Mom only had my best interests in mind, so I just smiled at what he said. I didn't mind wearing a small ringing bell around my neck, but I came to know today that apparently male dogs weren't supposed to wear them.

Mom told him about the time that I had gone missing in the house, and how stressful it was for everyone to search for me. She said that with the bell around my neck ringing whenever I moved, they wouldn't lose me again.

My uncle laughed. "So this *ghungroo* is his GPS!", he exclaimed. "Say whatever you want...", Mom replied. "...but he will have to wear this bell around his neck until he grows up."

My uncle admitted defeat and said that since I was her dog, Mom knew how to best take care of me.

The children came to see their uncle, happily wishing him a good afternoon, calling him "Mamaji". I didn't know what that meant, but I knew that it had something to do with their relation to each other. He seemed to be a dog person, because he took me onto his lap and pampered me a lot, talking to Mom about the do's and don'ts of raising dogs which Mom listened to carefully. Maybe it meant that I would now be pampered more. He stayed with us for some more time, eventually leaving to go to his office.

Chapter 18

Mysteries Solved

I had been noticing that Mahinder and Meena used to address Mom and Papa as "Madam" and "Sir". Mom and Papa, however, used to address each other as "Suno", so I often used to get confused and wonder how their names worked.

"Were both of them named "Suno"? Can a woman and a man have one common name? Was this their real name?". The more I used to think about this, the more confused I would be.

One day, mom's mother came to visit us. We welcomed her into our living room, where she kept her bag aside and took a seat on the sofa. In the meantime, Mahinder brought a glass of water for her. After finishing the water, she kept the glass down. She took a brief pause, maybe to regain her breath, then she asked Mahinder to call their madam. Soon Mom, Garima and Madhav were there before Garima's grandmother. As soon as she saw her daughter, she hugged her and asked her how Mom was doing and how her health was. Mom said that she was fine. Oh!- I played back Granny's words in my mind. My thoughts stopped at the word 'Neelam'. So mom's real name was Neelam! Finally, I came to know mom's actual name- Neelam. "If her real name is not Suno, but Neelam, then Papa must also have a real name, but what is it?"

Both Garima and Madhav were very happy spending time with their Granny, so I also sat beside her. She didn't ask the children anything about me, so I found her behaviour towards me very cold. The children, on the other hand, were telling her stories about me, but she didn't show much interest. All of them kept talking about one topic or another for the whole day.

It was now evening and Granny wanted to leave, but she waited for papa. After some time, Papa came back from the office. When Granny saw him, she happily asked him how he was doing.

"Wow, mummy. What a surprise! I am fine and doing well", he replied.

She told him that she was fine, too, and packed up her bag, getting up to leave. Papa interjected, asking her why she was leaving so early and to stay longer.

"Sorry, Rattan, but I was only waiting for you. I thought it would be rude to leave without meeting you. I've been here since the morning, and I really should go now. It gets difficult for me to drive when it's dark. Bye, Neelam. Bye, kids. Bye, Rattan."

"Rattan"! I thanked Granny for revealing Papa's real name to me. Papa was "Rattan" and Mom was "Neelam"! Finally, the mystery behind the whole "Suno" situation was close to being solved. One question still remained, however. If they knew each other's real names, why did they not call them by their names?

"Suno, I have prepared something special for you. All of you. Please change your clothes and come to the dining table", mom said as I wondered what the answer to my question was.

Papa left and went to change his clothes, and then Garima asked a question as if she had read my mind.

"Mummy, why do you call Papa 'Suno'? Even in this day and age, you talk to each other like a traditional Indian couple. Why not say each other's names?"

Mummy didn't answer, she just smiled and went to the kitchen. Garima's question was satisfying to hear for me, because it showed that I was not the only one who had this question in mind. I thanked Garima for solving the mystery of their names for me.

Though the mystery of names was solved, there was still one question which used to bother me a lot. I often used to think about why it was that I was sent to a new place and why I was called back the very next day. Soon it became clear to me when I saw Garima teasing Mom.

"Mummy, you don't feel giddy anymore now that Sultan's back? We never wanted to send Sultan away, but you were adamant. You were telling me not to think too much about him, saying that I should shift my focus away on something else, even though you yourself couldn't stay away from him even for twenty-four hours. Tears were flowing down from your eyes and you were about to collapse in the absence of Sultan." Then she had a hearty laugh and Madhav joined her.

When Papa walked in and heard this, he intervened.

"Garima, Madhav. Don't make fun of your mother. She was having a sleepless night when we had sent Sultan away.

She was crying all night. I even offered to send someone to get him at two in the morning, but she declined, saying that whoever we send would be cursing us for making them go at such a strange time. She waited all night, until morning. It's not something to make fun of. We loved Sultan from the start, we were just reluctant to take on a lifetime of responsibility."

When both of them heard this, they apologized to both of their parents, and said that they would never make this mistake again.

This is how I came to know the reason behind me being called back. I felt very relieved to know that my love with this family was not one-sided, rather, it went both ways. This thought definitely eased my pain. Besides, I wanted to forget that episode of my life altogether.

Chapter 19

I Fell Severely Sick

After many days, our mother ordered Chinese food for the entire family from their favourite Chinese restaurant. "Chowmein" and chicken "momos" were bought, and when they were brought into the living room and opened on the dining table, they smelled very nice. A delicious aroma had spread around the room and my mouth had already started watering. I wanted to taste the food so bad! Garima and Madhav tore into the food, eagerly eating the noodles and momos. Mom wanted to give me a momo to eat, but the Madhav was against the idea of giving me even a single one.

"Mom, he's too young for Chinese food, and this food is not meant for dogs, it is for humans. Don't give him anything to eat. Besides, thus stuff has ajinomoto in it, and that can be very harmful to him."

Mom protested, saying that she would only give me one, asking Madhav what harm one momo could do to me. Garima then joined Madhav's side.

"Mummy, Madhav is right. Don't give him Chinese food, it's really bad for him. Just one drop of poison would be enough to kill someone, but giving him this food would be like giving him a whole glass of it. Have mercy on him."

I was getting irritated over the arguments given by both of them, feeling like they were very selfish. They were devouring such delicious food and weren't letting Mom give me even one momo! I looked at the dining table, which was full of bowls of all kinds of delicious-smelling food.

"Garima and Madhav, you're both so selfish! You want to finish all the food... can't you share just one piece of your momo with me?" I thought to myself. I didn't know the momos were because this was my first time seeing them, but I knew that they smelled amazing and I wanted one.

I felt very happy when Mom ignored their advice and gave me one momo. It was incredible! I wanted to have more but, in the meantime, a shocking development took place. When Madhav saw Mom give the momo, he angrily left the room and Garima was also displeased. When my mother saw this, she couldn't gather the courage to give me some more food and I had to satisfy myself with just one momo. I still kept sitting near the dining table but to no avail, as they had finished everything, so I got on my bed with a heavy heart.

I think barely an hour had passed when I started feeling a slight pain in my stomach that grew with time. Everyone was sleeping, so I didn't want to disturb anyone. By midnight, the pain in my stomach became severe and I started getting painful cramps. I wanted to tell everyone that I was in trouble, but how? I somehow passed a painful night, and now I understood why Madhav was against the idea of giving me even a single momo. I was regretting eating Chinese food. It was so dangerous! Maybe I was too young for that kind of stuff, but now there was no use regretting my past mistakes. I somehow passed a few hours, while eagerly waiting for everybody to wake up and take me to the doctor.

I realized just how sick I was the next morning, I had a bad stomach and my motions were very loose and frequent. I felt very weak and low and now I had realised how a single momo had played havoc with my stomach. Now it was clear that I shouldn't have eaten it, but it was too late for this realisation to be of any help. I saw why Garima had compared that food with poison, and I was paying a heavy price for my temptation. Madhav and Garima were already very annoyed with Mom and now they had started blaming Mom for my poor condition.

I wanted to tell them that it was not her mistake, that she only gave it to me out of sheer love. I tried to convey this to them but they didn't understand my language at all... Mom looked and felt very sad and guilty, so much that she even apologised to the rest of the family.

Papa told her that it was not her fault, and that she only did what she did to empathise with me, then telling her to not waste any time and to take me to the hospital. I was glad to hear that someone in the family understood Mom's intentions.

She asked Meena to get ready and put my things in a bag and went into her room. It hardly took a minute for her to get ready and soon after, she came back out and we were ready to leave. While waiting for her, Meena was holding me on his lap and holding the bag at the same time. Mom asked him to give her the bag but he refused and adjusted the bag on one shoulder. He asked her if we were going to Tis Hajari hospital, to which she said yes. We went down and sat in our car, Mom asked the driver to take us to Tis Hajari Court and we then set out for the veterinary hospital. It took us lot of time to reach there!

After reaching there, she requested the doctor to see me urgently because I was in real trouble. The doctor was very nice, and he asked the others to wait for some time. Then he tended to me and asked mom about my problem. She told him everything in detail. The doctor examined me and told mom that I was suffering from 'parvovirus.'

He gave me an injection and prescribed some medicines. Meena left for the medical store, while we remained in the hospital. After some time, he came back with the medicines and showed them to the doctor. He called Mom and gave her some instructions for the medicines.

Mom noted down his instructions on the prescription paper and after keeping the medicines in the bag, the three of us started walking towards our car which was parked near the gate. When we were about to sit in our car, Meena brought something up to Mom.

"Madam, we should let him go potty now. What if he feels some trouble in the car? I'll take him to an isolated corner so that he can freshen up".

Mom said thanks to him for giving this idea. I was surprised that Meena could understand my needs so well, so I thanked him in my heart.

He took me to an isolated corner and I relieved myself there, peacefully. Then he put some sand on it so that no one could soil their feet in it. He also cleaned me with tissue paper, and then we went out and sat in our car. After some time, I once again started feeling very miserable. While going back, I was also finding it difficult to control my motions, but we were getting delayed because of a terrible traffic jam.

Somehow the driver manoeuvred the car cleverly and succeeded in coming out of the jam.

After much delay, we finally reached our colony. I was feeling relieved to be back because during our whole journey I was struggling to keep my motion under control. I was now having severe cramps in my stomach. We entered the lift and soon we were on our floor.

I heaved a sigh of relief!

Chapter 20

My Treatment at Sanjay Gandhi Veterinary Hospital

After entering the house, Mom put down me on my bed. To my surprise and dismay, I soiled it within a few minutes. I just didn't have the energy to move even an inch, so I had made my bed dirty. When Mom saw this, she panicked, because I had never spoiled my bed before. Not even when I was just a few days old.

She immediately rang up Bhanwar Singh and asked him what to do, telling him that the medicines weren't working and that I had just dirtied my bed, something I had never done before.

I was also feeling guilty for making the bed dirty, but I was helpless. My strength had been drained entirely. Bhanwar Singh spoke to Meena, whom he must have given some instructions to. He told Mom that they will take me to Sanjay Gandhi Veterinary Hospital and that Bhanwar Singh will join them halfway there.

"Bhanwar Singh knows somebody there and he has spoken to the doctor about Sultan, so they will attend him urgently. Do not worry about Sultan, Bhanwar Singh has told me that it is a very good hospital and the doctors are very competent," Meena said to Mom. Even his words couldn't give solace to mom, and she was still looking nervous and worried. I had never seen her so upset, so I also got worried.

Then Mom asked Meena to quickly make my bag ready. The bag was already with him, so he just added a few more things in it and we started for the hospital. After about half an hour, Bhanwar Singh joined us at the designated point. He spoke to me gently, saying back what had happened to me. He also patted me on my back and when he was seated, the driver started the vehicle again. It was a long journey and I was once again feeling like I was sitting on a swing, and soon I was fast asleep.

I woke up when the car had stopped. They picked me up and went to the doctor. The doctor said to Bhanwar Singh to tell him everything and spare no detail, so he could make an accurate diagnosis. Bhanwar Singh asked Meena to come forward and he explained everything. He told the doctor about the momos and the other veterinary doctor. He also said that I had never made my bed dirty before today. The doctor asked Meena to keep me on the table, Meena did as he was told. The doctor examined my stomach and said that I was suffering from an acute stomach infection. He told Bhanwar Singh that I had to be admitted for the day and that I had to be put on a drip. Soon, a sharp metal thing was put on my foot and fixed with tape, and I was thus put on a drip. I was also given some injections through the drip so that I wouldn't feel pain.

The hospital was very big, and many other dogs were there for treatment. There were two-three foreign doctors treating animals. I wondered if they had come to India just to serve animals. I really appreciated their dedication and commitment to the animals. I was put on the bed, which was close to the window. Bhanwar Singh started to talk to me about the different animals there.

"Sultan, look at the animals outside. I think you already know about cats and dogs. That big white animal is a cow. The other big animal there with black colour is a buffalo, and the bird with green wings there is a parrot."

I felt very happy to see three new species of animals, and I found the parrot very beautiful. The hospital was taking care of many street dogs, all of whom were suffering from various problems.

The doctor kept seeing me from time to time and in the evening, he talked to Bhanwar Singh about my condition.

"You have to make sure that he is not given anything to eat orally. He will remain on medicines and glucose only. His treatment will continue for three days. Once you bring him back tomorrow morning, and he will remain here till late evening. You can take him home now."

I remained there late into the evening. Bhanwar Singh kept sitting by my side for the whole day. Meena was not allowed inside, so he had to wait outside. When I was discharged, Bhanwar Singh called Meena inside, who picked me up from the bed and took me towards our car. When all three of us were seated, we started for home. By the time we reached back home, the sky had become quite dark.

Everyone was eagerly waiting for me, and I got a warm welcome from everyone. I could still see a pang of guilt on Mom's face. She said sorry to me. I wanted to tell her that there was no need for her to feel guilty, if she was responsible for my sorry condition then so was I. Preparations had been made for my arrival, my bed was laid on the floor and I was put to bed.

Soon I saw that Mom was spreading out a thick sheet near me, but I didn't understand why. Then I saw that she came close to me and laid down next to me. Then she pulled me close to her body.

"There's no need to do that, he can sleep alone," Papa said to her when he saw her. "You should come and sleep on the bed."

Soon he got a reply from Mom, which perhaps he had not expected at all. "Do we leave our children alone when they are ill?" she replied. "Have we ever left our own children alone whenever they had fallen sick? Should I let him sleep alone because he is not my biological child?"

I was amazed and happy that I had found my mother, my *real* mother. As she hugged me and slept with me, I felt the warmth of a mother's love. Her very touch was so soothing and pain relieving.

Today I had understood the actual meaning of her words when she said that even a puppy will be raised like her own child. I was so overwhelmed by the care and love I was getting from the whole family, that I now realised that I was an inseparable part of it.

Chapter 21

I Got My Real Parents

After two or three hours in the night, I had soiled my bed again. I was feeling ashamed of myself for doing this, but I was helpless and had lost control over my stomach. Mom had realised that something was wrong so she consoled me and said that I shouldn't feel guilty, and that it was ok. "Can she really read my mind?" I wondered. "Who told her that I was feeling guilty? How does she know my feelings if I didn't share them with anyone?"

It was a pleasant surprise for me, and her words helped me to come out of my guilty feeling. I felt a little relieved. My mother got up and switched on the light, then she opened the almirah and pulled out some cotton from a bundle.

After this commotion, Papa had also woken up and asked what was going on. Mom told him everything.

"Don't worry, it will be difficult for you to handle him alone so I'll help you. Both of us can manage together."

Then they took me to the bathroom and Papa cleaned me with wet cotton while Mom was holding me. While they were cleaning me, Mom asked him, "I am quite surprised with this sudden change in your attitude. Earlier you didn't want me to sleep me with Sultan, now you have volunteered to clean him. Why?"

Papa said, "Neelam, today your words have made me speechless, your words were so thought provoking. I was compelled to think that could I have left my biological child alone in this situation? Your words have shaken my soul so I came forward to clean him. I will always remember your words, we will raise him together."

I was so overwhelmed and became very emotional to the extent that there were tears in my eyes, tears not out of sorrow but out of my happiness, which knew no bounds now. I thought, "Wow! I had got my real parents now. I was a proud dog child today. Today father was not my father for namesake but now he truly became my father. I was happy to get both my parents." I thought that usually puppies have their mothers only with them but I was lucky to have both the parents. A complete family!

My illness had given me my mother and father both, this illness proved to be a blessing in disguise. Now I had a complete family, I already had a brother and a sister, now I had both my parents, my real parents. So now I was a happy puppy indeed. Wasn't I ?

Chapter 22

Super Tasty Daal

I was given drip for three days, I used to go to the hospital in the morning and come back late in the evening. I was getting more and more love on my arrival. I, then wished, "Jaise mere din phire vaise har kutte ke din phire."(Just as my days have changed, every dog's days should change.)

Bhanwar Singh told Mom that I had to be given only boiled moong daal water, just three to four spoons in a day. Next day when I got up, I was feeling very very hungry, to the extent that I could feel the pangs of hunger in my stomach. I was eagerly waiting for the food, suddenly I got a call from mom for my food. I was expecting very small quantity but to my surprise my small bowl was almost half full. I ate to my full satisfaction, when I had finished I realised that Mom had not followed Bhanwar Singh's instruction. Perhaps Mom had realised that I must have been very hungry because medicines couldn't replace food. So she gave me some more quantity of Moong Daal and gradually increased the amount.

This satiated my hunger, I still remember the taste of that daal. I found the moong dal super tasty because I had not eaten anything for the last three days. Papa was keeping a strict watch on my health as the kids were also doing that, very soon I recovered fully and started gaining strength also.

After a few days, Amar Singh came to our house and I got afraid that he had come again to take me to another place. Soon I felt that I was grossly wrong because he had come to our house to show some papers to Papa. Papa took the papers, after reading them carefully, he returned the papers to Amar Singh. I heard, Papa was telling him that he had seen many loving and caring mothers but he had not seen a caring mother like my Mom.

Amar Singh was surprised and looked anxiously at Papa. Then Papa told him about that night, when I had come back from the hospital and how mom slept with me the whole night. He said that the words she had used were so powerful that even his heart also changed for Sultan and how both of them cleaned me together. Amar Singh also became emotional and looked convinced of Mom's love for me, he said, "Sir, I had grossly misunderstood madam, when she had called Nawab back from my relative's house. Now I know that she genuinely loves him and really, she can't live without Nawab. I understand her feelings well. I have no regrets about my image among my relatives after listening to you. Earlier I was very annoyed with madam but not now."

I also fully agreed with him, I myself felt fortunate to have Mom like her. Suddenly Papa started laughing and told Amar Singh, "His mom has changed his name now, she has given him a new name 'Sultan'. So you can call him as Sultan." Then Amar Singh also smiled and said that definitely it was a better name, he also said that my new name suited my personality well.

It seemed that after listening to Papa, Amar Singh no longer held a grudge against Mom. He said to Papa, "Sir,

Sultan should be happy, it does not matter whether he stays with my relatives or with you. It is good that both madam and Sultan are happy with each other, this is more than enough for me."

Amar Singh's words made me thankful that he had excused my family.

Chapter 23

Pranayam and I

Mom used to do some breathing exercises in the morning in the balcony. Since I used to get up very early, so I used to follow her and reach the balcony. She would play music and would do some breathing exercises. I couldn't understand the meaning of those prayer songs but gradually I started picking up the words and their meaning, only a little bit. Mom used to do one very funny exercise, in which she used to exhale with a sound for a long time that too, continuously. I used to wonder what kind of exercise was that.

Anyways, I was only interested to sit on her lap, I was least interested in her exercises. I wanted to be around her all the time and wanted to spend most of my time in her lap. I therefore found this time best as only two of us would be there at this time … just two of us! I would thoroughly enjoy the warmth of her cozy lap. Whenever I would sit in her lap, it used to give me immense pleasure, I used to feel as if I would be on cloud nine.

The prayer songs she used to play, were sung in a shrill voice. I often used to wonder, "How can Mom enjoy these prayers in such a shrill voice?" Though initially I found the voice very harsh but soon I started liking it because my mother liked it. One prayer song she particularly liked, I had realised this because she used to play that song again and again.

Since I daily used to listen to those prayer songs so gradually I also started developing taste for those songs. After breathing exercises, Mom would sit quietly with closed eyes and used to do meditation. In the winters she used to wrap me in her 'Naga' shawl, carefully keeping my face out so that I could breathe easily.(Naga shawl is made in Nagaland) Her exercise used to go on for about forty-five minutes, meditation for fifteen minutes. After an hour we used to enter the room, where she would put me under the quilt, with Garima and Madhav.

Once, I heard, she said to Garima, "Garima, today I couldn't do my Pranayam properly so I am feeling very uneasy." This is how I came to know that these breathing exercises were known as 'Pranayam' and these were integral part of Mom's life.

After doing Pranayam she would take a bath and get ready, to go to her workplace and would come back in the afternoon. Every day she used to enquire about me, from Meena, that what did I do in her absence? Meena used to give a detailed report of my activities and Mom would listen everything with keen interest every day.

This used to make me feel that I was very important for her.

Chapter 24

Pigeon-Poop and I

Papa used to take me for a long morning walk to keep me fit but I had picked a bad habit. I had started eating a particular thing, wherever I would one. The first time Papa saw it, he immediately told me not to eat it. "No, Sultan! That's dirty. It's pigeon poop. Don't eat that", he said.

I didn't eat it for the rest of the walk, but I was back at it again the next day. This time, when he saw me, Papa scolded me.

"Sultan! I told you yesterday that you shouldn't eat that. Stop this right now."

This time his tone was stern, and it scared me into stopping.

"Papa must be thinking that I should stop this habit altogether," I thought to myself. I wanted to stop, but I couldn't resist it. On our way back home after finishing my walk, I promised myself that I won't eat the pigeons' poop again.

When we were on our morning walk again the next day, I forgot the promise I had made to myself and ate the poop again. Papa yelled at me to stop when he saw me, but this time I felt no fear from his tone. He still tried to get me to stop.

"Sultan, please leave this habit. What you're eating is very dirty. It could upset your stomach and make you sick. Be a good puppy and do as I say", he said to me.

We continued our routine of going for a morning walk but I was unable to stop myself. One day, when we came back, Papa finally took a stand. He took up the phone and called someone.

"Bhanwar Singh? I used to consult Amar Singh whenever I had to ask a question about Sultan, but he's retired. Can you help me with my problem?"

He paused, probably to hear the other person's answer, and then resumed talking.

"Sultan has developed a very bad habit. When I take him out for his morning walk, he eats the pigeon poop on the ground. At first, he listened to me, but now he keeps doing it until I can pull him away from it. I've been thinking that I should put a muzzle on him to make him stop… is that a good idea?"

After hearing what Papa said, I hung my head in shame as I wondered why I was unable to break my habit. Why couldn't I stop myself?

I don't know what Bhanwar Singh said to Papa, but there came a small change in our routine after that phone call that brought about a big change in my behaviour. The next day, when we were about to leave for my morning walk, Papa went to the kitchen and kept something in his pocket. When we left and reached the ground floor, Papa gave me a small piece of a dog biscuit. I got so busy munching the biscuit that when we walked forwards past some pigeon poop, I forgot all about and didn't eat it. After all, I already had something tasty in my mouth.

Papa now made this a standard practice. Whenever we would near any pigeon poop, Papa would give me a piece of a dog biscuit. In some time, I had completely overcome my dirty habit. I felt much better and much less guilty now that I had stopped.

Several days later, Bhanwar Singh came to our house in the morning. Papa and I were sitting in the living room when he came in, and he handed a file over to Papa which he carefully read and signed. He then asked Papa about me.

"Sir, has Sultan changed his behaviour now and stopped eating the droppings?"

Almost before he completed his sentence, Papa told him his idea was wonderful.

"Your method showed results right from day one. Now he doesn't even look at the pigeon poop. But tell me one thing: what was the harm in using a muzzle?"

Bhanwar Singh smiled as he answered Papa's question.

"Sir, we should always take positive actions to change bad habits. A muzzle is a negative measure because with his mouth completely enclosed, Sultan could have become aggressive. That's why I recommended biscuit therapy!"

"You're very convincing", Papa said. "I just couldn't think of the side effects of using a muzzle. Thank you for that bright idea."

Bhanwar said that he was glad his advice proved helpful. He sat there for some time and then left, having given us the very useful tip that if we want to change someone's habit, we should use a positive method instead of delivering punishment.

I said immense thanks to Bhanwar Singh for helping me in getting rid of a bad habit.

Chapter 25

A Pleasant Coincidence

One day, Uncle Devesh came to our house to visit us. He asked Meena to call Mom, and as soon as she entered the room, she hugged Uncle Devesh and asked him to take a seat.

"So how are you Devesh? How are the kids and Hitha?", she asked him.

"Everyone is fine Didi, and so am I. Where's Sultan? I'm eager to see him," he replied.

"Haven't you noticed? He's sitting right next to you."

Mom then went near the big sofa and picked me up, much to Uncle Devesh's surprise.

"Oh My God! He's so black that I couldn't even see him or make out his face."

He then took me on his lap and caressed me. As he did so he told Mom that I was a street dog and not a Labrador, but Mom didn't care.

"He may be a street dog or a Labrador, but he's ours, Devesh. His breed doesn't matter. If he really was a Labrador, then I could have thought of giving him away to someone. Now that we know he isn't one, I won't give him away because I can't stand the thought of a family abandoning him when they learn about his breed. I'm happy to have him, and happy that you and Hitha motivated me to bring him back."

When I heard her, I, too, became thankful to my uncle and aunt, and was quite surprised to hear that. Mom asked my uncle a question.

"Devesh, I remember you saying that you were taking care of a big dog. How is he now?"

Uncle Devesh seemed a little said as he gave Mom a reply.

"Didi, he was so big that he needed a lot of space, but all the families willing to adopt him were living in small flats. I asked Dr. Hussain, our neighbour to adopt him, and he readily agreed. He has a big farmhouse in Rudrapur, so I personally went there to drop that dog off."

Mom then asked him another question.

"By the way, how did you come upon that dog?"

"His owner was probably just using him for breeding and when he became old, his owner must have thought him to be useless and just abandoned him. He clearly had no street smarts and must have been attacked by street dogs. I remember him being badly wounded with maggots in his wounds... I came upon him when he was lying near our house and yelping in pain. We went outside to see what was making those sounds, and there he was, in terrible shape..."

He continued, "...we brought him in and cleaned his wounds, and then we called a vet to see him. It was the vet who told us that the dog was only used for breeding. He gave us some medicines and ointments, which we used to treat him. Didi, Hitha used to have to remove maggots from his body herself, one by one."

It was clearly not a pleasant memory for him, and he was silent for some time after taking a deep breath. Mom asked him what was wrong.

"I wonder how some people can be so selfish and cruel", he said. "Whoever did that to that dog kept him around as long as he was making money, and then threw him out like trash."

Mom consoled him, "This world has people of all kinds, Devesh. Just like how it has people like that cruel breeder, it has people like you who selflessly take care of animals that are complete strangers."

With his spirits seemingly lifted, he started another conversation after a brief pause.

"Didi, I have surprising news for you. The day after I came back from Rudrapur, a German Shepherd came to Kavita Didi's house. He seemed to be familiar with the place because he seemed to know where he was going as he was moving. He only stayed there for one day and one night, and the next morning when Kaanan was on her school bus, the dog moved with the bus but then just disappeared. Vikas was saying that it surprised him because one second he was there, but then the dog was just gone in a blink."

Mom pointed out how all three siblings had encountered dogs in similar conditions, and wondered out loud if it was a coincidence or a gift from god. Uncle Devesh replied that he had no idea.

I also believed like Mom that it was definitely not a coincidence but there was a difference between those two dogs and me. They couldn't live with uncle and aunt's families whereas I became an integral part of my family.

My good luck indeed!

Chapter 26

Nicky and Cherie

One day Mom said to me that our aunt, Hitha had invited us to their place. Mom told me, "Your aunty has invited you to their place because she is keen on seeing you. Your uncle has told her so much about you that she is curious to meet you. Soon we will visit their place." After a few days, we started for Gurgaon to meet my aunt. Mom picked me up and sat in the car. She had kept some old newspapers also in the car, I thought that she will read them to pass her time. When we had just entered Gurgaon, I realised that I wanted to pee urgently. First, I tried to control but when I had failed, I started whining.

My Mom understood that I wanted to pee so she spread the newspapers on the floor, then she gently kept me on those newspapers. Then I came to know that she had kept them for this purpose but I didn't want to soil our car so I kept whining, Mom then understood that I won't pee in the car. Finally, she asked the driver to stop the car immediately, by this time I was desperate to get down and relieve myself.

Finally, the car stopped, Mom put me on the pavement and I peed there. She felt proud of me and said to the driver, "See, he is so intelligent, he is so small despite that he didn't pee in the car. He didn't soil his car, he has smartly conveyed us this message." When I heard this I also felt proud of myself, Mom took me on her lap and started caressing me. Very lovingly...! I liked this very much and took this gesture as my reward and felt very happy. When we reached my Mom's parents' house, aunty started showering love on me. I thought, she was also a great dog-lover like her husband.

Mom was served tea and snacks, both Mom and aunty sat down on the sofa. Aunty said to mom, "Didi, (elder sister) Sultan has reminded me of my dogs Nicky and Cherie, they were very naughty." Then Mom asked aunty to tell her about her pets and both of them gladly sat down on the dining chairs. Mom said, "Tell me in detail so that I come to know about dogs more. Sometimes, I get anxious whether I am taking good care of him or not, this is absolutely new experience for me. Though we had a pomerian pair, Jiny and Johnny, when we were children but our mother used to take care of them so we didn't learn anything about dogs."

Aunty said, "Didi, there is nothing that I can enrich your knowledge. I only have hilarious things to share with you, Didi, when I saw Sultan, suddenly the sweet memories of our dogs have become alive. I would love to share those with you." Mom said that she would love to hear that.

Aunty started narrating about her dogs and said, "Didi, Nicky and Cherie were too naughty and they always had new ideas to implement to. I, Rohit (her brother) and the two dogs used to sleep on one bed. Whenever we would get up in the night to go to the washroom, they used to occupy our pillows and we would spend the whole night without pillow. There used to be a virtual war for the pillows, we used to try to snatch from them and they used to become more adamant to keep it under their custody. We always used to lose in the fight for pillows."

She added, "One more very interesting thing was that that they were very fond of eating chocolates. Since it was not good for them so we hardly used to give them chocolates but they were also very clever. Whenever my father's sisters used to visit us, Nicky and Cherie would never allow them to enter the house till they would get chocolates from both of them. We used to find this very interesting, one day my Mom told my aunts that chocolates were not good for them. So they shouldn't bring chocolates for the dogs and they agreed. Once both my aunts came to our house, when the door was opened for them, Nicky and Cherie started barking at them."

She continued, "Since my aunts were instructed by my Mom not to give any chocolates to them so they had not brought any. So the dogs kept barking and didn't allow them to enter our house. Finally, everyone gave up and Mom asked my aunts to get the chocolates. Poor aunts, they had to go to the nearby shop and get chocolates for them and when the dogs got the chocolates, only then, they allowed aunts to enter."

Mom had a hearty laugh on listening to this and kept laughing for quite some time then she finally said, "Hitha, I have never heard about such clever and smart dogs. It was really very funny story you have told me. I will take care that Sultan does not become fond of chocolates."

Mom took her lunch with her family members, aunt gave me some milk and soft bread to eat. When Mom had finished her lunch, we sat there for some more time while mom was having a chitchat with the other members of the finally. After some time, Mom expressed her desire to leave and we started for our house.

I had also found Nicky and Cherie's deeds very hilarious.

I kept laughing in my heart for quite some time.

Chapter 27

Gabbar and I

We were living in Flat Number 3-A and Jasmine aunty and her family were living in 2- A. They had a dog, Gabbar, who was a golden Labrador. We had become friends through Garima since she was very social and an expert in making friends. She had made friends with Gabbar's family, too. They must have asked her to take me to their house, so she started preparing to visit Gabbar. She persuaded Mom to accompany her and she readily agreed, and so both of them took me to Gabbar's house in the evening.

We were given a warm welcome by aunty, who asked Mom and Garima to have a seat. When she saw me, she lovingly said, "He is so small and cute, Garima! You have brought a lovely puppy. He has reminded me of Gabbar's childhood. How much did you pay for him?"

Garima said, "Aunty, we've not purchased him, I just found him on a road. He was in terrible condition and I wanted to save his life. I felt that the best way was to bring him home, so I brought him home with me, that's all."

Aunty became curious to know more about my story so Garima narrated everything to her. She was very surprised to hear it. "You really did a great job, Garima. If only more people were sensitive to the needs of animals like you are", she said.

I took a look at Gabbar and saw a huge blonde Labrador dog. It was probably time for him for evening snacks. Their helper brought two bowls for Gabbar, with chicken soup in one bowl and snacks in another. I smelled the aroma of soup that had spread throughout the entire room and had an irresistible urge to drink the soup. It smelled so delicious! I quickly ran like an arrow towards the bowl, finished the entire soup, and then devoured the snacks next to it. Before Gabbar could react and bark at me, I quickly ran and hid under the sofa, which he couldn't enter because of his size. Gabbar got annoyed and started barking at me very loudly. I could hear the anger in his voice. I was feeling very scared! My heart was pounding out of fear but I knew that I was safe under the sofa. Now I was regretting my greed, when I sensed that great danger was looming around me in the form of Gabbar. There arose a ray of hope when I heard Jasmine aunty's voice.

Jasmine aunty intervened and called her domestic helper. She said, "Get more soup for Gabbar, quickly. He's starting to get aggressive."

The helper hurriedly went into the kitchen and brought some more soup for Gabbar, which pacified him immediately. The moment the bowl was kept on the floor, Gabbar got busy drinking his soup and then Jasmine aunty pulled me from under the sofa and started caressing me with affection.

Though Gabbar didn't like my greedy act, he forgave me and started licking me and we became good friends. I had realized that it was not just that Gabbar had a big body, to me he had a big heart, too.

Aunty told my family that Gabbar was suffering from acute arthritis and cataracts. She said that he was not taken out to get fresh, he was using a small bathroom for all of that. Aunty said that it used to pain him a lot whenever he was taken outside to get fresh, so the family had trained him to do it all inside the house. I was very pained to hear about Gabbar's health issues.

We sat there for some more time and then left for our home. Mom started scolding me for my stupid act, she said, "Sultan, what will they think about you? They will think that we don't feed you enough so you devoured Gabbar's soup. You are very greedy, learn to control yourself, especially when you are outside. Do you want to bring a bad name to your family?" I was feeling very sorry for what I had done so I promised myself that I would learn to maintain some control over my gluttony.

From that point on, Jasmine aunty started calling me often to their house to give company to Gabbar. She had also started taking precautionary action whenever I visited their home. She had started keeping a separate bowl for me, to avoid any kind of unpleasant scene. Perhaps Gabbar used to eagerly wait for me because he always greeted me when I came. One day, Jasmine aunty asked Garima to come with me. They started sharing their experiences with Gabbar and I. In the end, Jasmine aunty said to her, "Garima, Gabbar has given us so much that we can never forget and repay him."

When I heard this I thought, "How and what can a dog give something to his family? It is the family that gives something to the dog and not vice versa."

Though I couldn't understand what Gabbar had given to his family, it was clear to me that Gabbar was indeed very precious to his family. So was I!

Chapter 28

Apple Parties

It was a holiday for all the family members, so everyone was at home. Papa and I were eating our share of apples when suddenly Mom happened to come into the kitchen. When she saw us, she had a hearty laugh and said, "Oh, both of you are busy having an apple party. What a scene!"

Papa replied, "You can join us, it will be our pleasure." Mom said, "I have not had a taste for apples right from my childhood so I can't join you but I do have a question. You were born in Jammu and Kashmir, a place best known for apples, so it is natural for you to have a liking for apples. But Sultan was born in Delhi, so how come he has developed taste for apples just like you?"

Papa replied, "I thought about this many time myself, but I never came up with a satisfactory answer. Anyways, I just wanted to thank you for buying these apples." Mom just said thanks and left the kitchen. I also said thanks to Mom in my heart for making my every morning a happy morning with an apple.

When I was a baby, I used to eat a lot. I could eat anything in any amount. I used to eat apples, tomatoes, carrots, cucumber, papaya, banana, water-melon, musk-melon, eggs, oranges, biscuits and many other things, but apples were my weakness. Around 5 in the evening, I used to get another fruit to eat. My life was full of eatables and I was becoming a glutton. I didn't mind becoming one as it was fun eating a variety of things. I used to eat all that besides my three regular meals.

After eating so much, I used to feel a lot of pressure in my stomach and I used to make heaps of potty on the balcony at night. Mom used to clean it up early in the morning with a long green pipe. I used to watch her from the net door, watching her expression intently. I would anticipate seeing a feeling of disgust show up on her face but she always surprised me because I never saw her making a face or frowning. It made me marvel at her patience. I used to feel very guilty whenever I would see Mom cleaning up after me but I was always helpless when it came to having control over my stomach.

What a mother is, I would think! When I grew up and controlled my diet, I got better at controlling myself and stopped making my balcony dirty, finally stopping my guilty feeling.

Chapter 29

I Stole Aloo Paranthas (Stuffed Potato Bread)

One day, I saw Mahinder and Madhav talking to each other.

"What would you like to have for breakfast?", Mahinder asked him.

"*Aloo ka parantha,*" he said.

Mahinder happily went into the kitchen and got busy in the preparation. When Mahinder had finished making them, he placed two aloo- paranthas on a plate and put lots of butter on them, just how Madhav liked it. He kept them on the small center table and then told Madhav that his breakfast was ready. Madhav then went to the washroom to wash his hands.

Mom was sitting on the dining chair, busily doing her schoolwork as I was sitting beside her. The intense aroma of paranthas had filled the living room and my mouth had started watering. I couldn't resist having those paranthas, so I stealthily looked at Mom and found that she was engrossed in doing her work. I took advantage of this and quickly ran towards the centre table, jumping onto it and devoured those paranthas in one big gulp. After that, I quickly ran back towards Mom and sat down there quietly as if nothing had happened. I tried my best to look normal and was feeling very happy that I had fulfilled my desire without coming to anybody's notice.

I had hardly realised that Mom had witnessed everything! I didn't know that she had seen me quickly jumping onto the centre table and gulping down those paranthas without any concern for how hot they were! When Madhav came back, he saw that the plate was empty. He sat down on the chair and must have thought that his breakfast was not ready yet. After a few minutes, he grew impatient and called out Mahinder.

He yelled out and asked Mahinder how long it would take to make his food, asking him to hurry up and saying that he was very hungry. Mahinder sounded perplexed as he replied and told Madhav that he had already put his breakfast on his plate.

"The plate is here, but where are the paranthas?", Madhav said in an agitated tone.

Mom then started laughing, and Madhav asked her what she was laughing at.

"Madhav, your breakfast has been eaten by somebody else," she said smilingly. She had seen my greedy act, so she told Madhav about what she saw. I was terrified because I was expecting a scolding or a beating from Madhav, but he was to forgive me quick, joining Mom in laughter. It was a huge relief to me.

Madhav asked Mahinder to make more paranthas for himself again, keeping a strict watch on both me and his plate this time. He was guarding his paranthas and plate carefully. I thought that my family was very kind and empathetic to overlook my mistakes so easily. Now I realise that I was very greedy when I was a puppy.

After this incident, Mom instructed Mahinder to always make one small parantha for me as well so that I wouldn't attack other's food. She also asked him to give me whatever was prepared for breakfast in small quantity. This became a standard practice and it is followed till today, so I don't feel like everyone is getting something and I'm not. I feel very satisfied when I get to eat what my family members are eating, it adds a lot of variety to my food and tastes amazing.

I had many a times taken a vow to keep my craving under control but my vow used to miserably crumble under the weight of my taste buds! Alas!

Chapter 30

A Visit to Mrs. Lalchand's House

My Mom had a very close friend named Mrs. Lalchand and when she came to know that my family had decided to keep me with them forever, she came to see me. She liked me so much that she took me up on her lap and gave me many compliments. Very lovingly, she gave us an invitation to visit her in her home, which my mother gladly accepted. The next day, I was taken to Mrs. Lalchand's house, with Meena carrying me as Mom walked behind us. The fear of Mom disappearing and abandoning me crept into my mind again, and this thought was very scary to me.

"Maybe she wants to abandon me", I thought. "Maybe that's why she is not carrying me."

I tried to look back to see if she was coming or not, and I started whining to try to get her attention. Meena seemed to be quick to understand my feelings, so he advised Mom to keep pace with us until we reached our destination. Once we had arrived, he dropped me off at Mrs. Lalchand's house and went back home. Mom pressed the bell and we were welcomed by a shrill bark from behind the door. Our host, Mrs. Lalchand, opened the door, greeting us and asking Mom to take a seat.

She had a white female Pomeranian dog who looked very stylish and well-groomed. Mrs. Lalchand had kept dog biscuits for me and some eatables for Mom, and after exchanging greetings, we started eating. As I was eating, a glass somehow fell down with a crash on the floor. It scared me so much because of how sudden and loud it was, so I quickly to Mom and jumped up into her lap.

"Kids feel safe with their mother whenever they are scared," She said to Mom.

"It's the same for him. Look how quickly he jumped on your lap when he thought he was in danger."

Mom nodded her head in agreement and started caressing me. Mrs. Lalchand was right, I felt completely safe in Mom's lap.

The white Pomeranian's name was "Flunky". The name suited her well, as she proudly flung her butt side to side as she walked. We sat there with her for about an hour, during which Mrs. Lalchand kept playing with me and patting me. Flunky didn't seem to like this, however. She seemed to dislike the idea of Mrs. Lalchand showing so much love to a stranger puppy, but Mrs. Lalchand didn't seem to understand.

She had given us a lot of snacks to eat, and I was overwhelmed with her generosity. I didn't understand why Mom was holding back and not eating much, but I made the most of her generosity and devoured as much food as I could. It satisfied my stomach, if not my desires.

After some time, Mom told Mrs. Lalchand that it was time for us to leave.

"Madhav will be home anytime now, and I want to be there when he arrives", she said. Mom and Mrs. Lalchand said their goodbyes, and we got up to walk to the door and leave. When Mom opened the door, Meena was already standing there to carry me back home. I wondered why Mom didn't carry me around herself. Why did she hesitate? Was she somehow ashamed of it?

As we were walking towards our flat, Mom ran into a friend of hers, "Sushma". Mom and Sushma said hello to each other and had a brief chat. After their brief talk, they said goodbye to each other and we continued walking back home. Once we arrived and walked in, we saw Madhav already sitting on the couch in the living room. As soon as he saw me, he happily ran towards me and started playing with me. Mom smilingly told him to change out of his school uniform and eat his lunch before playing with me, telling him that I was not going anywhere. After playing with me a little more, he went into his room to do as Mom told him and change his clothes.

Seeing Sushma refreshed my memories and I went into a flashback.

A few months ago, when Mom was looking for a family to adopt me, I remember her ringing someone on the phone at one point.

"I have a black dog and I'm looking for a family fond of dogs who will take him in. If you have any relatives who are interested, please let me know."

After putting the phone down, she happily went and told Garima that Sushma's daughter Jia wanted to adopt me. She said that Jia would soon come to Delhi to meet her parents and adopt me.

A few days later, Mom used the phone again to call Sushma and ask about Jia's arrival. After putting the phone back down, she looked sad and disappointed. When I saw the expression on her face, I became a little worried for her. Since I had heard her say Sushma's name over the phone, I figured the issue must have been about my adoption.

After the whole Gurgaon village episode and my homecoming, Jia came to Delhi and visited us in our home. She was given a warm welcome by Mom and Garima. Mom asked Meena to bring some snacks for Jia to eat, but she politely refused.

"No formalities needed, Aunty. You're treating me like a guest who has come from afar. I live in the same colony as you, just two blocks down."

Mom just smiled and said "Okay."

I walked in and happily jumped onto Mom's lap.

Jia was overjoyed to see me and quickly picked me up off of Mom's lap, putting me on her own.

"Wow... he's so cute! Mummy had told me about him, but he's even prettier than she said. I've come here to take him with me to Amritsar, Aunty."

She kept lovingly playing with me.

"You'll be just like a little brother to me, cutie! We'll be together after a few days."

I looked at Mom and Garima, and they both looked speechless when they heard Jia. They were looking at each other as if they were asking each other, "What now?"

Mom gathered her courage to say something to Jia.

"Jia. I'm very sorry to say this, but... I can't give Sultan to anyone now. We've decided to keep him here, with us forever. He's become an integral part of our family."

Jia did not seem pleased to hear this.

"Aunty, you yourself proposed that I come and take him with me. I planned this whole trip just for him. Please don't disappoint me like that now that I'm here. If my mother said anything to you, it was without my own opinion having been considered."

"I wish you had discussed your trip with me, Jia. I wanted you to adopt Sultan because I know how much you love dogs. Your mother agreed initially, but later on, she declined. I had already given him away to an unknown family after that, but I just couldn't stay away from him so we called him back to us. Now we can't separate him from our family. I really do feel sorry for you, but it's not my fault."

Jia looked even more disappointed, and a little desperate.

"Aunty, please try to understand my point. I'm facing a lot of problems in my life right now. I consulted an astrologer and he said that the planets *Rahu* and *Ketu* are causing me these problems. If I feed or keep a black dog, the planets will be pleased and my problems would come to an end. So please... give me your dog and help me out."

"Jia... I understand your problem, but believe me, what I have just told about Sultan and our family is true. We can't think of giving him away to anyone. That's final, Jia."

"Aunty, I'm sure that I can't get such a beautiful and adorable puppy in the market."

I think that Mom saw that this argument wouldn't come to an end, so she firmly and politely said that she couldn't give me to anyone. Jia looked very sad, stayed in our house for a bit longer and eventually left.

I wondered how a black dog could solve someone's problems just like that.

"How can a black dog please planets?", I thought. "Is a black dog just that strong? Do the planets love black dogs so much that they decide to end the problems of pet parents?"

These things were beyond my comprehension, so I never came up with an answer.

Chapter 31

The Importance of Dogs in Indian Mythology

The next day, Mom, Garima, Madhav and I were all sitting in the living room when Garima asked Mom a question.

"Mummy, how can a dog solve someone's problems in life? Why was Jia so keen on taking Sultan with her? How could he solve the problems she's dealing with?"

This question made me alert and piqued my interest because I also wanted to know more about this. I was excited to have my questions answered. Mom immediately opened her laptop, typed something and started reading.

Mom gave a very elaborate answer to us both, and she fully sated both Garima and my curiosity.

"Dogs, especially black dogs, are very important in Indian mythology. A black dog is the mount of Lord Bhairav and always accompanies him, so they're thought to be blessed and it's considered auspicious to have a black dog."

She told us that it was tradition in Hindu families to prepare two *rotis* first, one for a cow and one for a dog. Only then could the rest of the family make and eat their own *roti*. She also told us that when she was a child, she had seen her grandmother feeding a female dog after she gave birth to puppies. It used to be standard practice to take care of the mother dog so that she could feed her puppies well. If a family was unable to feed her, then another family would volunteer to take their place. This was how the entire community would look after mother dogs.

"Dogs are worshipped in parts of Sikkim and North Bengal. Sometimes they are the mounts of scary-looking gods, sometimes they guard important places like the entrances of heaven and hell. In Hinduism, dogs are associated with Lord Shiva."

Mummy talked about a special dog called "Sarama", who was called the mother of all dogs. She said that Sarama even helped the gods find their stolen cows one time.

She also talked about Yudhishthira, who she said was someone important from the Mahabharata. He asked the gods to give a dog who followed him through many trials a place in heaven, and that dog turned out to be some god called "Yama", who was testing Yudhishthira's truthfulness.

"Speaking of Yama, he is said to have four dogs with four eyes guard his domain. Because of how important they are to him, dogs are sometimes considered a link between the netherworld and Earth."

Mom also told us that an astrologer had advised her that if possible, one must keep a pet dog. He added that the dog is one of the most faithful animals, with the horse being next in line. If a family decides to keep a pet, they must keep him for his entire life, because it would be very cruel to abandon the dog halfway.

According to this astrologer, a dog can sense when his family might be in danger and wouldn't hesitate to take the trouble on for himself or even sacrifice his life for his family.

He said that dogs provide positive energy to the house where they live and take the negativity out of it.

Garima and Madhav both looked very enlightened once Mom was finished. They thanked her for telling them so much about the importance of dogs in Indian mythology.

"I gotta say that I never imagined that dogs would have so much importance in Hindu mythology. Dogs basically have superpowers!", Madhav exclaimed.

I now understood why Jia wanted to adopt me so badly. She could have bought a puppy from the market if she wanted one. But she pretended to want me because of how cute I was, actually, she didn't want to spend any money.

If I really could ease someone's problems, then my family would come first. I would use any superpowers I had, to protect my loving and caring family. They cared so much for me that I would repay them whenever I could. Why should I solve a stranger's problems?

My family was not in the mood to please anyone, and neither was I.

Chapter 32

My Toys

Garima had bought many toys for me. Some were balls, one was a small stuffed monkey and the others were stuffed toys. The monkey had small ears and a very long tail, it looked cute and was my favourite. Garima would play with me by throwing the monkey and I would run to and bring it back. I had fun chasing and bringing back the balls she would throw, too. The balls used to make an interesting tapping sound when they bounced but I still liked the monkey the most, to such an extent that I used to sleep with it next to me. That monkey was very cute and its long tail was very fun to play with. Garima used to hold the monkey by its tail and keep held at a height. Seeing it hanging just in reach above me made me jump to bite it, and this is how I learnt to jump high and higher. After grabbing it I would hold it in my mouth like my prey and shake it all over, which was very satisfying.

I had one small teddy bear, a few balls and a small calcium bone to chew. The bones were very juicy and soft, the more I chewed them, the softer they became. They helped me when I was still teething because it was very soothing to bite down on them whenever I felt pain in my growing teeth. Garima had also bought two small puppy toys with moving heads, which Mom kept in the front of the car. I always enjoyed watching their heads bobble around like they were bouncing on water.

One day, my entire family went to dine out in the afternoon. Before leaving, Madhav told me that he didn't want to leave me alone but that he couldn't help it because dogs were not allowed in the restaurant.

"Don't worry," he said. "I'll bring you a gift when we come back."

My family members came back after a couple of hours with a surprise for me. Madhav had kept his promise and presented me with a very big ball. I started wondering how I would play with a ball so big that I couldn't even bite it.

"Sultan, this ball isn't like the others you have."

Garima explained to me how I was supposed to play with the new ball.

"This is a football. You're supposed to kick it, not bite it. We'll teach you how to play."

Madhav took the ball and started rolling it with one leg. He gave it a push with his foot and sent it towards me. I now understood how I was supposed to play with it, and I tried to roll the ball with my leg. It worked on the first try! I was overjoyed to see that both Madhav and Garima had started playing football with me. I liked the ball very much and playing with it was very fun, even if it was too big for me to fit in my mouth!

Later on, Garima taught me how to kick the football. She used to drag the football first then she would kick the ball. When she repeated this several times, I also learnt to do this. After teaching me how, she asked me to come forward and kick the ball myself. I tried to drag the ball with one leg but when it was time to kick, it didn't work! My leg just slid against the ball without moving it. Garima asked me not to lose heart and keep practising some more. I followed her advice and kept trying, and eventually finally succeeded in kicking the ball again. When Garima saw it, she gave me a big round of applause and patted me on my back.

Then she requested all the family members to come to the living room, and she didn't forget to invite both Mahinder and Meena. Soon, once all of them were in the living room, Garima asked me to kick the ball as they watched. When I saw the entire family looking at me, I became nervous and my legs started shaking a little. Garima lovingly patted me, which calmed me down a little as I moved to kick the ball again. I moved my leg close to the ball and when it was almost touching, I pushed my paw forward with a lot of speed, hitting the ball and making it move. When everyone saw this, they clapped a lot for me so I felt really proud of myself that day. The applause had taken my motivation to a new level, and I now felt ready to learn some more football skills from Garima.

I was overjoyed to get such a big applause, my tail started wagging vigorously out of happiness and this had made my day.

Chapter 33

My Gender and Milk Teeth

One Sunday morning, when all the family members were home, I felt the strong urge to pee so I went running to the balcony to relieve myself. Madhav was already sitting there when I arrived and started peeing near the drain, unaware of the fact that Madhav was observing me keenly. He suddenly got up and went running to Mom and said in a shocked tone, "Mumma, our Sultan is not a male baby. She is a female! Garima lied to us about her gender."

My Mom was surprised to hear this so she asked him why he said what he said, telling him that I was definitely a male and Garima was telling us the truth. Madhav made a smug face and said that he had just seen me "peeing like a female dog", saying that there was no way I was a boy if I peed the way I did.

Though I didn't know the meaning of female, I, too, believed him for the time being. My mother had a hearty laugh.

"Madhav, listen closely. Just as it is difficult to distinguish between male and female human babies by their voice until they hit puberty and get older, dogs, too, change when they get older. Sultan is a baby now. Once he reaches his teen years, he will start to pee like a male dog. Until then, male and female dogs pee in the same way."

Madhav looked relieved and believed Mom, asking her how long it would take me to be more like a boy.

"Probably five or six months", Mom told him.

Now completely satisfied, he didn't raise any more questions and went back to his room with a learned expression on his face. When I grew up more, I started peeing more like a male, instinctively raising a leg as I did it. My gender was never an issue to me, but it was nice to see the issue resolved anyway. It made me more confident in my identity.

Some days later, I woke up feeling like one of my teeth was wobbly, and I also felt a little pain somewhere in my mouth. I quietly sat down on the floor and Mom happened to walk in. She started caressing me, but noticed some blood on my lips. She then opened my mouth and found some blood on my gums. It made her very anxious, and she started checking the floor around her, soon finding a broken tooth on the floor. From its size, she realized it was my tooth, and she looked even more worried than before, calling out to the others.

"Look here! Sultan's teeth are falling out and there's blood on his gums! Call a doctor!"

Papa said, "First let me enquire from inspector Bhanwar Singh, if he advises us to consult a doctor, we will do." He took out his mobile phone and spoke to Bhanwar Singh. He told Bhanwar Singh about my bleeding gums and broken tooth. In the meantime, both Garima and Madhav came running to me to show their concern for my broken tooth, they were consoling me that I shouldn't get worried. They also promised me that they will consult a good doctor.

When his conversation was over, he had a relaxed expression on his face. He told the entire family, "There's no need to panic, Bhanwar Singh has told me, just as human babies' milk teeth fall with the passage of time. The same happens with puppies also so relax it is absolutely normal." I saw my family members, they too, were satisfied.

Suddenly Mom said, "I will always keep his tooth with me. He is my little baby and I couldn't keep my childrens' teeth but I will keep it with me forever."

I felt so fortunate and lucky when I heard this. I wondered, "Why mom loves me so much." I just didn't have any answer to this question.

Chapter 34

My Shortlived Training

Life was going on very smooth, I used to enjoy each day with lots of eatables and playing around with toys, running around here and there all the time, with that monkey toy. I was a free soul as my family had never tied me with a leash. No one had ever yelled at me or hit me even with a paper, in short, I was the apple of their eyes. I used to move around freely and used to consider myself as one of the happiest dogs in the world.

One day an unknown person came to our house and Mom introduced me to him. I couldn't understand that why she did so. Later on, I came to know that he was my trainer. He had been called to teach me basics which a dog should know. After some time, he started giving me training, he was teaching me to fetch newspaper but it seemed a useless exercise to me.

I thought, "Papa brings the newspaper whenever he comes back from the walk. Moreover, Mahinder and Meena were also there to bring the newspaper. Why I should be trained to fetch the same, when three persons are already there to do such a tiny work then why the trainer is bothering me so much." So I didn't show any interest in learning that exercise and this had perhaps annoyed my trainer a lot.

Since I was not following the commands of the trainer then he made a small roll of paper and hit me with that. I immediately ran to my Mom and jumped on her lap out of fear. He came following me, made his voice sugary and tried to persuade me to come down but I did not budge. Perhaps Meena had seen him hitting me so he immediately brought this to Mom's notice. She frowned and angrily asked the trainer, "Why you have hit Sultan, we don't even shout at him. Hitting is not acceptable to us."

The trainer gave his justification, "I didn't hit him hard and it was just a roll of paper, how hard I could hit him with this." Mom didn't seem convinced, she requested him, "Please try to understand, he is a little puppy and is apple of our eyes. Hitting him can have bad impact on his psyche. So please be gentle with him." He replied, "Madam, training requires some discipline so I have to be little tough with him. You will have to bear with this." Mom reluctantly said o.k.

Then he gave another ghastly and deadly idea and said. "Madam, I think you have been very soft with Sultan throughout. In that case I can take him out for training because I have to be a little tough with him." I was sure that Mom won't give such permission but I was wrong. I was surprised with shock that Mom agreed to this idea very easily. The trainer looked very happy with Mom's approval and said that he would come tomorrow for my training. OMG! Again. This boring, monotonous and strict training.

Surprisingly Meena came to my rescue like an Avatar, he said to Mom, "Madam, if the trainer can beat Sultan in our presence, what he would do downstairs when we won't be there, who is going to keep an eye on him, neither you nor me. If he says that he would be tough means he can beat Sultan severely." When Mom heard this, it seemed as if she woke up from a dream. She said to Meena, "Why this did not click to me. How could he convince me so easily? What a fool I am."

Now when Mom seemed convinced, she said, "You are right Meena. I don't know that why I couldn't understand hidden meaning of his words. You are smart to judge him rightly, we don't want to get Sultan recruited to police or army, so why such rigorous exercise. We should teach him some basic manners, this will be alright." She immediately rang up the trainer and asked him to discontinue my training from the next day. I thought to myself, "Thank you, Meena brother. Thank you so much."

This is how my training came to an end, to my pleasure.

Chapter 35

A Powerful Chamaat (Slap)

One Saturday afternoon, Granny come over to our house and I found out that she was going to stay with us for a day and a night. Throughout her stay, she repeatedly asked my family members to keep me tied down, asking Garima several times to put me on a leash and keep me in a separate room. She also got mad at me jumping up and down from the bed and sofa as I wanted.

Everyone tried to convince her that it was how I was brought up and that they couldn't just suddenly tie me up to something and leave me in one place. The more I ran about and moved around the house, the more irritated she got. She shouted at me many times and asked me to stop running, but I didn't care to listen.

"My mom was here. Why should I listen to someone else or worry about what they're saying?", I thought to myself. This was my house, after all, and not Granny's. I was the Sultan of this house. I continued doing what I wanted.

The next morning, when everyone was sitting in a bedroom, something terrible happened to me. Garima and Madhav were doing their homework and Granny was reading the newspaper while sipping her tea, with Mom sitting next to her on the bed. When both of them kept their teacups down, I jumped up on the bed from one side and ran and jumped down from the other side. It was fun to do, so I did it a few more times.

Granny got angry and asked me to quietly sit still, complaining about me to Mom.

"Mummy, he's just a baby. He's full of energy. What is he doing to bother you reading your newspaper? Let him be a kid and play."

Granny was not having it.

"Don't make me beat you. Sit quietly and stop being naughty."

I didn't care what she said. No one in the family had ever harmed me and Mom was sitting right there to make sure I did what I wanted. She was so protective of me that just a few days ago, she had shown the door to a trainer who hit me just once with a roll of paper. After all I was Sultan of our house.

Once again, Granny insisted that I stop moving about, but I didn't listen to her. When I was on the bed and near her, ready to jump back down, she pulled me by my ear and gave me a powerful slap right on my right cheek! I was numbed by shock, because it was so unexpected and unbelievable to me that someone had hit me. It was as if I had entered a vacuum.

A complete silence spread in the room as Garima and Madhav stared at Granny with shocked faces.

Mom shouted at Granny.

"Mummy! What have you done!? You hit such a tiny baby just for playing around? We don't even raise our voices at him and you raised your hand against him! That's too harsh!" "A slap on him is a slap to my heart, mummy. I will never forget; how cruel you have been to my little baby Sultan."

"I did the right thing. You've spoilt him. He has no discipline. Someone has to teach him some manners. Is this how he would behave around guests? I regret nothing."

There were tears in my eyes but I hid them, "If I show her my tears, my Mom would be hurt more. Better I turn my face in some other direction." thought I.

I came back to my senses after a few minutes and realized that Granny was more powerful than Mom. She could hit me and Mom couldn't do anything. I went to sit near mom quietly, having lost any desire to play. Maybe this was for my own good? Granny, meanwhile, was boasting about disciplining children.

I decided to call her Beating Granny. No, ..., SUPER Beating Granny. It was the perfect name for her. Her picture got deeply imprinted in my heart. I had started dreading her, deciding to avoid her whenever she would come to our house in the future. I was sure that I will never be able to forgive her in my lifetime. Never ...

Chapter 36

A Neem and Methi Daana Bath (Fenugreek Seeds)

I think Mom had a liking for natural things, I remember that she never gave me packed food as it might contain some preservatives. Although Bhanwar Singh had suggested a herbal shampoo for me, Mom had decided to give me a bath with water boiled with Neem leaves and fenugreek seeds so she asked Mahinder to bring Neem leaves. The next morning, Mahinder came back with lots of neem leaves which Mom was very happy to see. She said to Mahinder, "Wash these leaves, then take two big bowls of water. Boil this and leave it till colour of the water changes to green. Don't forget to add fenugreek seeds in the water."

Mahinder curiously asked Mom, "What is the benefit of this water?" Mom replied, "Mahinder, both the things are anti-bacterial, these will kill all the germs and bacteria. They are also good cleansers so why we should shampoo which contain chemicals? Our preparation is absolutely herbal and safe." Mahinder looked satisfied with the answer, he accordingly prepared herbal water and strained it, then he kept the bucket under the fan to let it cool down.

Mom put cotton in my ears to prevent the water from entering my ears. By the time the water had cooled down, I was taken to the balcony. Then Mahinder started scrubbing me with the leaves, which was very soothing. Though Neem water was very bitter to taste, it smelled very refreshing. When they were through, I was wiped down with a towel. Once I was thoroughly dry I was taken out for a walk. Mahinder brought me back after half an hour and I was given a mashed boiled egg on my arrival which I enjoyed very much.

One day, Mrs. Lalchand came to see me, she was quite impressed with my soft and shiny jet black fur. She said to Mom, "Sultan has such bright fur, it shines like anything. I have never seen such a shiny dog with such thick and jet-black hair. I think you should take him to some dog-show, I am sure that he would bag first prize." I felt very proud of myself but I knew that the credit goes to my Mom. Mrs. Lalchand asked Mom, "Which shampoo do you use for Sultan?"

Mom said to her, "I don't like shampoos which contain chemicals. I prepare neem water for his bath, I don't even trust herbal shampoos." Mrs. Lalchand curiously enquired about the whole procedure of preparing the Neem water which Mom explained gladly. Mrs. Lalchand said that she would also give a bath to her Flunky with the herbal water. As usual, she showered her love on me and gave me a biscuit which I devoured in a few seconds. Then the two ladies had a chit-chat for a while, after which Mrs. Lalchand expressed her desire to leave.

Before leaving, Mrs. Lalchand reminded Mom about the dog show. I was very excited to go for the show and bag a prize for the family but my Mom politely turned down the idea and said, "Leave it Mrs. Lalchand, he is made for us, we aren't interested in showing off him to others." I liked this idea as well but Mrs. Lalchand didn't agree with Mom and she still insisted that I should be taken to a dog-show.

In the evening the railway phone rang up, indeed it was Mrs. Lalchand. She spoke to Mom and said something which I couldn't hear but I saw a smile on Mom's face. When their conversation was over, Mom kept the phone down and started laughing. She told me, "Sultan, it was Mrs. Lalchand's phone, she told me that she also gave neem water bath to Flunky. You know she is white in colour and she became green after the bath. I forgot that you are black so green leafy water wouldn't affect you, whereas Flunky is white. It just did not click with me that Flunky could turn green."

Then my mother started laughing again and I did too but there was difference in our laughter. She could laugh with an expression and sound whereas I could laugh only in my heart. I was imagining the pure white Flunky turning green. I knew that I was becoming mean, I shouldn't have thought this at all but it was just a thought and came to my mind. I did not deliberately think of this.

Oh, I was thinking that now Mrs. Lalchand should take Flunky to a dog show, she would definitely bag first prize for being the first green dog of the world!

Ha ha ha, green Flunky! Wow!

Chapter 37

My Sweet Dreams

One day, when she was talking to me, Garima told me that Mom had left her school job and had started working for some company from home, on her computer. I felt very happy to learn that she would stay home all day because I could now sit on her lap for as long as I wanted.

After eating breakfast, she went to the computer room and sat on the chair to start working. When I saw her go in, I followed her and looked up at her expectantly, wanting her to put me in her lap, and I started whining when she didn't. She immediately understood and picked me up, putting me down right where I wanted to be. However, because of the way she was sitting, I was slowly sliding down constantly. Mom kept having to stop me from falling further and putting me back in the center of her lap. She eventually just put me back down for my safety, but I started whining again. She picked me up again a little later, but moved her left leg to make more room for me in her lap. I hardly realized how difficult that pose must have been for her to maintain, but she did it anyway just to keep me happy.

It became part of my routine for me to spend time on her lap until it was time for lunch, when she would go eat lunch and have a nap before resuming her work while keeping me on her lap. I didn't realize that I had developed a craving for snuggling with her. Even when she was reading the newspaper on the sofa, I would jump up on the sofa with her and make my place on her lap.

One day, as Mom was reading the newspaper, Pawan happened to come in to collect Papa's briefcase and saw me sitting on my favourite spot.

"Madam, I always see Sultan sitting in your lap. Does he just love it that much?", Pawan asked.

"He's my little baby, so he loves being in my lap."

Pawan smiled, took the briefcase and left. I think he was right to say that I was always in Mom's lap, because I was also in her lap in the early mornings when she would do her breathing exercises, too. Whenever a guest would come to the house and Mom would sit on the sofa, I would make the most of the occasion and go sit in her lap. It just made me feel warm and safe.

I used to have a lot of dreams where I would sometimes just be in her lap. Other times, I would be eating all sorts of things. Apples, watermelons, eggs, chicken… my dreams used to be full of food! Sometimes, I used to dream that I was running after some street dogs whom I was chasing away, or a cat that I was scaring off. I had no idea that in my sleep, I was moving my legs in a running motion just as I was in my dreams.

Mom told Papa about me moving my legs in my dreams when he came back from the office, and he laughed about it.

"At least he's running in dreams, if not in reality! I'm happy to hear he was running at all!"

I didn't like this joke, but I kept my displeasure to myself. Papa also used to complain that I would never bark when it was appropriate, which I found to be totally wrong. I barked at many appropriate moments. I barked whenever there was a delay in giving me my food. I barked in excitement whenever I was taken outside for a walk. I barked at Mom for giving me a biscuit as a treat. I also barked at people who were shady, which meant people who wore helmets and our gardener, both of whom were always suspicious-looking to me.

To me, these were the perfect occasions to bark.

"Should I bark more often at other moments?", I wondered.

"But when?"

I couldn't think of any other occasions that seemed sensible, and I saw no reason to bark at people unnecessarily.

Chapter 38

Our Helpers

I often wondered about all the helpers that would come to our house to do different chores. Dharmender used to come to clean our house, and I often heard him praising me, saying that I was a very good dog because I never bit anyone. He talked about someone he knew whom he called "Mishraji". He said that everyone who worked at this person's house has been bitten by their dog.

"One day, when I was working, I was scratching my leg because it was itchy, and the dog immediately bit my hand. He hasn't spared anyone who works there," he said.

I felt very happy whenever I heard him praise me. I would never be so aggressive as to bite someone, I was a peace-loving dog.

I also remember that Madhav would often play rough with me. He would often put his hand in my mouth, and Mom would warn him every time.

"Don't behave so rudely with him", she would say. "He could bite you."

Madhav would confidently reply by saying that he loved me so much that I would never bite him.

Mom would then tell him that that was because I was a very calm and quiet dog, and if I was any other dog I would have bitten his hand. She would tell him that he was taking advantage of my politeness and simplicity. I loved hearing compliments like that, and felt very proud of myself for not biting anyone.

Though we had Meena and Mahinder to cook for us, a new helper named Raamesh came to our house. He was very suspicious-looking, and I sensed something off about his character right away. When he would be doing dusting, he would look around with a shifty expression in his eyes, how I imagined a hawk flying above the ground would look when it hunted for an easy meal. I started keeping an eye on him to confirm my suspicion, and oh my god, I was right!

One day, I saw him stealing money from Garima's almirah. Another day, I saw him eating dry fruits from the kitchen as he cleaned it. Yet another day, I saw him steal a knife from the kitchen, and later I saw him steal Garima's expensive watch. It was shocking to see him brazenly take these things as if they had belonged to him from the start. How dare he steal my sister's watch?

Before stealing anything, he would send Meena and Mahinder away on one errand or another. Neither of them suspected anything, so they believed him, but I stayed at home. I would watch all his misdeeds. Even if he tried to hide, I would catch him with my sharp eyes. His crimes may have been hidden from some people, but they could never hide from my sharp eyes.

When Mom would come home from school, I would try to tell her what I saw, but she couldn't understand me. It was strange that I could understand her language but not the other way around.

One day, Raamesh took me for my afternoon walk. He was standing near the canteen when some street dogs came in our direction. I jumped towards them, but he was still holding the leash so he lost his balance and fell down. When he got back up he gave me a slap and brought me back home.

The next day, he told Mom that he had slapped me and was sorry for it, saying that it happened almost instinctively and that he wanted to tell her himself before someone else told her about it. She listened to him patiently, but didn't utter a single word. She had a very stern expression on her face. The next day, I learnt that he had been shown the door. I felt very happy because only I knew the truth about him stealing. Though the slap episode was unpleasant, it gave me immense relief that he had been shown the door. It was a blessing in disguise indeed!

Chapter 39

A Change in My Attitude

There was a change I noticed in my attitude. I was becoming possessive when it came to my Mom. I couldn't bear for any of the kids to get too close to her. I became aware of this one day when Garima came back from college, looking very tired. Mom was sitting on the sofa, and Garima was so tired that she dropped her bag on the floor, got on the sofa and put her head in Mom's lap. I was sitting on the floor in peace, but when I saw this I got very jealous of Garima. I jumped up on the sofa, where Garima's legs were. I tried to push Garima off the sofa, but she was too heavy for me, so I changed my plan. I wedged myself between the sofa and her, and slowly started making my way to Mom, slowly moving Garima away. It took some time, but I finally reached Mom's lap, having displaced Garima completely. Yay! She was all mine!

When I tried to remember how my attitude turned into this, I recalled a memory from many days ago. Mom had a disagreement with Madhav and Garima in the evening, which soon turned into a heated argument. This argument continued for some time, and they soon started quarreling over something. After some time, Mom was done talking. She said that she was going to sleep out in the balcony, and wouldn't sleep inside.

She angrily left the room and went to sit in the balcony, and I followed her and sat down beside her. I was determined to spend the night with her. It was so hot out in the balcony, however, that I started panting. Mom switched on the balcony fan, but it just moved around the hot air.

Soon, I was surrounded by mosquitoes. Mom tried to keep them away, but it didn't work. She picked up a newspaper and started fanning me with it. It was relieving for the time being, but there were more and more mosquitoes coming to me. Maybe my black fur was attracting them?

Finally, after an hour, Mom picked me up and went inside to protect me from mosquitoes, even though she intended to spend the night on the balcony like she told the kids.

When morning came, Mom brought up the night to Garima and Madhav.

"He's my only real child. He was sitting beside me all the time. Neither of you bothered to check on me or call me inside, because of how selfish you are. I had to come inside because there were too many mosquitoes biting him. Even then, he didn't leave me alone. Neither of you wanted to leave the comfort of the A.C., but Sultan didn't care about that. From now on, he's my real child."

After hearing her, I grew possessive. I started thinking that only I deserved her love, no one else.

Both Garima and Madhav expressed regret about what happened the previous night.

"We wanted to come to you, but we were afraid that you would scold us. We didn't want to hurt you. We're very sorry, Mummy. Can you forgive us and forget this?", Garima said.

After this incident, I couldn't tolerate it if Garima or Madhav tried to take my love. I didn't care about their apology. If Mom said that I was her only child, then I was her only child.

Chapter 40

A Street Dog Hurt Me

It was late evening when Garima and Madhav took me out for my usual evening walk. We walked in the dog park for about half an hour, and by that time it had become dark. They took me near the canteen, and Madhav went inside to buy something. Garima and I waited outside for him, when suddenly a pack of street dogs appeared out of nowhere and started barking at me. I gave them a befitting response, after which they became very aggressive and ran towardsv me! One dog bit my nose with his sharp teeth right before I ran away and hid under a parked car. It was terrifying to see such wild and violent dogs. Garima started shouting for help.

"HELP! Save our dog, someone!"

When Madhav heard her, he came running out of the canteen. Thankfully, many people came to my rescue. They started picking up and throwing pebbles at the dogs, eventually succeeding in chasing them away. Some people consoled Garima and Madhav.

"We will drop you off at your block safely", one of them said.

"Carry a stick next time to scare the street dogs away", another suggested.

We started walking towards our block. The helpful strangers kept their promise and dropped us off near our block. I was still trembling with fear, and my heart was beating very fast. Garima and Madhav were still in a state of shock, and neither of them uttered a word as we were walking. I was so terrified that I didn't even notice that my nose was bleeding. Madhav noticed it when we reached the lift and the light inside shone on me. He pointed it out to Garima.

"Oh my god. Garima, look at his nose. It's bleeding. He must be in so much pain..."

Garima was also shocked when she saw it. When we reached home, she started crying bitterly.

The parents walked in and saw me, and they were worried, too. Papa asked Madhav what had happened to me. While he explained, Mom hurriedly brought cotton and a disinfectant. She cleaned the wound with the lotion and then applied some medicine on my nose.

Garima was clearly feeling very guilty that she couldn't save me from the street dogs. She was pleading to take me to the hospital.

"It's O.K., Garima", Papa said to her.

"We love Sultan just like you do. You're terrified because you saw what happened to him, but think how scared he must be to be who, it happened to. If you keep crying, he will only get more scared. All the hospitals are closed right now. If the bleeding still doesn't stop until morning comes, we will definitely take him to the hospital."

Morning came, and Mom noticed that my nose was still bleeding. She immediately asked Meena to make my bag ready, and told him that she was going to take me to the hospital, and that it was urgent.

She took me to the hospital we always went to. We waited in the line, and when it was our turn, Mom narrated the whole thing to the doctor. He cleaned my wound, gave me some medicines and an injection after that.

"He's going to be fine now. I've given him an injection to work against rabies. The bleeding will stop soon, and the medicines will help with his pain a lot. You can take him home now."

We left for home, and by the time we had arrived, I already felt the medicines working. When Garima came back from her college, she was very happy to see me, as was Madhav.

"I'm happy that the bleeding has stopped, but I'm worried that this wound might become a permanent scar on my Sultan's beautiful nose."

Hearing Mom say that, I, too became worried about my beautiful nose.

Chapter 41

Garima Got Hurt

Garima had taken me for an evening walk, and at one point she was holding my leash loosely as I was looking around. Suddenly, I noticed a cat run in front of me, and I instinctively jumped at it. I heard a loud sound as I jumped, and when I turned around I saw that I had pulled Garima and she had fallen to the ground with her weight on her wrist. I felt very guilty for being the reason for her fall and became quiet. She stood back up and took hold of my leash again. We went back home, but she didn't tell anyone about what had happened after coming back.

She did tell Mom the next morning when she complained about her wrist hurting. I was scared and thought I would get scolded, but to my surprise Mom didn't say anything to me. She just took Garima to the Railway Hospital while everyone else stayed back. I eagerly waited for their return, and prayed for Garima's wellbeing while I waited. On the other hand, I got mad at myself for causing her so much trouble.

They came back after about an hour. Papa seemed very worried for Garima, and asked Mom to tell him everything the doctor had said, which she did.

"He first asked Garima how it had happened. Then he got an X-ray done, and didn't find any fractures, only a ligament tear. So she has to wear a plaster for now."

I was relieved to hear that she didn't suffer a fracture, but I couldn't help but feel stupid.

"Why couldn't I control myself and stop myself from seeing some stupid cat? I have to be more careful in the future", I thought to myself.

I had learnt a lesson for good.

Chapter 42

Mysterious Shadows

It was evening, and all five of us were having fun on the balcony. There was a stand which we hung out clothes to dry. Out of nowhere, I started barking at the stand and at an unknown figure. Everyone was wondering why I had suddenly started barking and they were confused to see it. They asked me to stop, but I didn't. Something must have gone to my head because I was not listening to anyone. Garima saw a perfect opportunity to show her knowledge about dogs to the others and said that I might have seen a spirit or a ghost.

"What makes you say that? How do you know he's barking at a ghost?", Mom asked her.

"I've read it in books. Dogs can sense and see spirits that humans can't. I'm sure that there's a presence there that only he can perceive," she replied.

Papa just laughed and walked out of the balcony and into the home. Garima, meanwhile, tried to convince Mom that she was right by mentioning books and other things she's read. She was slowly swaying Mom to her side, who believed that there was no other reason to explain my barking.

Madhav, however, was not buying any of it.

"Mummy, why are you believing this nonsense? She's making a fool out of you and you're easily becoming one. There are a lot of things we don't know about dogs. Sultan could be barking for any reason. It's definitely not a ghost. Use your own common sense!"

Mom still couldn't decide whether to believe Garima or not. Madhav was annoyed to see that she was even considering it, so he got irritated and went back into his room. Mom asked Garima if it was a prank. She considered what she was going to say for a few moments, and then told her that she had seen it in many books and movies. She even names of few books and movies. It seemed that mom was convinced with Garima's arguments.

"Believe me or don't, but I have a strong belief in dogs being able to sense the paranormal," Garima continued.

Mom noticed that I had stopped barking but was still staring at the wall. She asked me and Garima to go inside. I was still confused about the cause of my incessant barking, and I still wondered about the mysterious shadows on the wall.

Chapter 43

A Visit to Faridabad

One day, Mom got an invitation for lunch from her sister. She gladly accepted, and excitedly told me that I would soon get the chance to visit another place and meet her sister. It made me very excited to meet her family.

On the day of the event, we went on a very long journey to meet Mom's sister. When we arrived, we were welcomed with open hearts. Garima's cousins were overjoyed to see me and started playing with me. The younger cousin was so excited to see me that he started peppering me with kisses.

"Can we please have him?", he asked Garima.

"He's so cute! I'd love to play with him".

Garima politely refused.

"Sorry, Amaan, but we can't give him to you. Whenever you want to play with him, you can come to our house."

He tried not to seem disheartened as he nodded, but I could see the disappointment on his face.

I had never seen their mother, Mom's younger sister, before. She had prepared food with meat for the guests. Everyone sat down to eat, and they praised her cooking skills the whole time.

"Anju, this food is amazing! The meat you prepare is simply delicious", Papa said to her.

Hearing all the other compliments the food was getting made my mouth water. It smelled so good! It broke my heart to know that I had to satisfy myself with the smells alone.

When everybody had finished eating lunch, she wanted to give me some pieces of meat to eat, but Mom was not keen on the idea of giving me spicy food. Mom requested that I not be given spicy food because it would upset my stomach. She was probably concerned that I might get sick again after eating something not meant for me. The last time was so bad that I now shuddered at the thought of having spicy food, but I still wanted to eat what everyone else was having. Mom's sister, however, insisted that I be fed.

"Neelam, think of how he must be expecting something for himself when everyone else is eating. Don't worry, I will rinse his pieces under running water to wash off the spices. He's just a puppy, after all. He can't control himself. Let's have him taste his aunt's cooking."

Mom didn't object anymore and so my kind aunt gave me a few pieces to eat. It really was delicious, and I thanked her in my heart.

Mom asked Garima and Madhav to clear the table, so both of them started picking up the plates and bowls. Their aunt, who I now felt was my aunt, too, started helping them. Garima and Madhav went into the kitchen with the plates and were about to throw the leftover food into the dustbin when my aunt asked them to stop. They looked back at her in surprise.

"What will you do with this leftover food and bones, Masi?", Garima asked her.

She told Garima that it was part of her daily routine to feed the dogs in her neighborhood and that they gathered outside when it was time to eat.

"They have become very fond of me and I of them", she said.

I admired her for what she did.

"Was mom's entire family fond of animals?", I had wondered before. Now I knew that the answer was yes! I was glad to be part of such a wonderful family.

Chapter 44

A Painful Morning

When I woke up the next day, I was unable to move my legs. There was a severe pain I felt there that made it so I couldn't even get up. I couldn't even move when Papa came to me to try to get me up for my morning walk.

He seemed to have sensed that I was having problems standing up, so he put me down from the bed. I tried to walk but I just fell back down. Papa became seriously worried and rang up Bhanwar Singh to talk to him about my problem. While he was on the phone, he took me to the balcony and put me up on a chair that had a net instead of a set, moving my legs around so that I could pee while staying on the netted chair. Even though it may have been possible, I still didn't want to pee like that. It was too uncomfortable.

Bhanwar Singh arrived at our house soon after. Papa brought him out onto the balcony so he could see me, and it shocked me to see him laugh when he saw me on the chair.

"Sir, I don't think it's anything to worry too much about. It's probably just a pulled muscle, nothing serious. I'll handle it easily."

He carefully lifted me up and massaged my legs thoroughly. It felt like the rest of my body was joining with my legs again. To my surprise, I could walk again after just a few minutes of being massaged. Papa looked very surprised to see me stand and walk around again.

“I don’t even know how to express my gratitude to you”, he said to Bhanwar Singh.

“It’s like a miracle. I can’t tell you how worried I was to see his plight when he couldn’t move, and you solved what seemed like an impossible problem in no time. I really appreciate it.”

Bhanwar Singh thanked Papa for the praise and offered to take me for my morning walk himself. Papa readily agreed, and so Bhanwar Singh and I left. When we came back, Mom treated him with breakfast. Papa thanked him once more, and he left with a proud feeling on his face.

A few days passed, and one morning I heard Garima telling Mom about a Military Hospital nearby. She said that they were known for treating dogs and giving them baths, and after telling her that they also treated civilian dogs, she insisted that Mom take me to them. Mom readily, agreed and so a few days later we left one morning with Mahinder accompanying us, headed to the military hospital Garima talked about.

After driving for about twenty minutes, we had arrived. The hospital had a big gate out front which was closed, but there was a smaller gate carved into the bigger one, and the smaller one was open. We got out of the car and I was immediately overcome with excitement for seeing an entirely new place. I instinctively ran towards the small gate at full speed, unaware that Mahinder was holding me on a leash. He had no idea that I would run so fast, and as I entered the gate I heard a loud *THUD*! I turned around to see that Mahinder had banged his head on the top of the small gate!

Silence spread throughout the premises and every eye was now on Mahinder. I thought that he would faint or feel giddy, but he kept standing. Mom sheepishly asked him if he was okay, and gave me a light slap at the same time. He didn't really look alright, but he tried his best to look normal and told her that he was fine. His words failed him as he struggled to keep his balance, but he put on a brave face and managed to compose himself. I felt very bad for him and got mad at myself for doing what I did to him. Mom asked him to drink some water and sit for some time.

Mom and Garima took a hold of my leash and walked on in, and once we were inside we stood in a queue. Once it was my turn, I was given an injection for something and then I was taken for a bath. While I was taking a bath, I saw many big animals there. They were too big to be dogs. Mom had also seen them and felt curious, so she asked a man standing nearby about them.

"Are these horses and camels sick? Are they here for treatment?", she asked him.

He told him that they weren't sick, but that they were from the President's house. He went on to say that they were there for training. I had never seen such huge animals in all my life, and it got me thinking about how big the President's house must be to fit such huge animals in it. In that moment, I wished to visit the President's house.

I wondered whether my wish will be fulfilled or not??

Once it was our turn, Mom showed me to the doctor. She told him about the pain I had in my leg some days ago and requested that the doctor should check me thoroughly.

The doctor examined me and told Mom what he had found.

"He seems to be suffering from arthritis. You should take the utmost care of him."

Mom and Garima were shocked to hear what he had said. Both of them looked very sad. I didn't know what arthritis was, but looking at the two of them made me sad, too. Was I suffering from some deadly disease? It was a terrifying thought.

Mom asked the doctor if there was any cure, and he apologetically said that there was no medicine that could cure arthritis. He said that all they could do was give me medicines that would "relieve the symptoms". It was the only way to give me some relief, he said.

We all headed back to the car with heavy hearts. Once we were sitting, Mom rang up Bhanwar Singh and weepingly told him about my diagnosis. I felt like crying, too. Was I about to die? It was too soon! I was too young to die! I didn't know what Bhanwar Singh said to her, but she had a more relieved expression when she put the phone back down.

Once we were home, I was surprised to see Bhanwar Singh already there, waiting for us. Mom started telling him about my diagnosis. I was listening intently. This was a conversation about my life, after all. Bhanwar Singh patiently listened to everything Mom said. Once she was finished, he said something surprising and relieving to her.

"That doctor is focussing too much on theoretical knowledge. We focus on practical knowledge. I've spent half my life with dogs. My experience says that if a dog has arthritis, the symptoms start showing within six months, and Sultan is around eleven months old. He's too young to have gotten arthritis at six months of age. The pain he felt back then was only a muscular pain and had nothing to do with arthritis." "If at all he has arthritis, he should have been still limping, but see he is moving around comfortably," he confidently continued.

His words seemed to relieve Mom of all her fears. She had more faith in Bhanwar Singh than in the doctor. I didn't know the meaning of arthritis, but I was very happy that I didn't have it. I heaved a sigh of relief, happy to know that I was not going to die from arthritis.

Everybody else in the family was very happy to hear those words from Bhanwar Singh, too. Mom asked Meena to serve him some tea and snacks and after finishing his tea, he asked for his leave. Papa came back from his office in the evening and Mom told him everything, what she had heard from the military doctor and what Bhanwar Singh had said. Just like Mom, Papa showed more faith in Bhanwar Singh's words.

"Once Bhanwar Singh said that Sultan had no problems, you shouldn't have looked for a second opinion and caused yourself so much tension. I think you wanted to have a professional opinion, but I trust Bhanwar Singh fully."

I was glad to know that I was not suffering from any serious problems. I could sleep without any stress.

Chapter 45

Flunky and Her Tussion

One day Mrs. Lalchand invited me and Mom to their house. Mom was holding my leash in her hands, when we were on our way to their house. It was indeed very pleasant surprise for me that Mom was holding me for the first time. When we reached our destination, Mom pressed the bell and Flunky responded with her shrill bark. The door was opened by Mrs. Lalchand, she welcomed us and called us inside. When mom was seated, she made me sit on another sofa chair. Flunky started barking at me, I couldn't understand the reason of her aggressive behaviour.

Mrs. Lalchand tried to make her quiet but she didn't listen. Mom asked Mrs. Lalchand, "Why she is barking so much on Sultan. She seems to be in angry mood today. I have never seen her barking at Sultan." Mrs. Lalchand hesitatingly said, "I don't know how to tell you." She took a brief pause and shyly continued, "Actually Flunky does not like if some other dog sits on the sofa or bed. She is annoyed to see Sultan sitting on the sofa."

My Mom started laughing but I didn't find this amusing at all. I was angry and I became determined to sit on the sofa only. I was quite surprised at her attitude, this was definitely not the way to treat her guest. I thought, "Does she think that other dogs are inferior to her?" She was still barking but I just did not bother and didn't respond. Finally, she got tired of barking and stopped. Hurray, I won!

We were served snacks and we got busy eating and Flunky jumped on the bed. Mrs. Lalchand told us that now Flunky wanted to wear sunglasses and Bindi (a small dot like sticker, which Indian women put on their forehead).

Then Mrs. Lalchand went inside a room and brought sunglasses and a Bindi. Mrs. Lalchand adjusted the glasses on her face and put bindi on her forehead. After wearing those, Flunky started giving poses like a model, she was so proud and conscious of her beauty. I saw all her poses and styles, befitting a female dog, with keen interest. She was looking really impressive in all the poses, when she was through with her modelling and fashion show was over, we came back home. I was served my lunch, though my stomach was full but I just couldn't say no to the food that was served to me. When I had finished, Meena took me for a walk.

After coming back, I went to enjoy a sound sleep with a bloated stomach.

Chapter 46

My First Birthday

Several days passed, and one day I woke up to Garima telling me that I will be one year old on the third of August. Both Garima and Madhav were very enthusiastic about celebrating my first birthday! They asked the parents to celebrate and throw a party for me, and Mom and Papa had readily agreed but they wanted the children to take the initiative. Garima and Madhav thanked them and told me that they had started planning my birthday party!

I didn't know what that was, but I understood that it was some kind of celebration. I was curious about the guest list… would my uncle and aunts be invited? As I was wondering who was going to come, Garima explained what was going to happen to me.

"Sultan, it was one year ago on the third of August that I had brought you to our house, which is now your house, too. You're very special to all of us, so on your birthday we will throw a party to celebrate you coming into our life!"

I spent the rest of the day anticipating my birthday celebration, and managed to sleep despite battling my excitement.

The next morning, when Garima and I were sitting in the living room, I saw her dial numbers on the phone and invite people three times. Once she was finished, she told me that she had invited three guests to my party.

"Happy!?", she asked me with excitement on her face.

I wasn't that excited.

"Just three guests?", I wondered.

"How much fun could I have with them? There should have been more people invited to my birthday party. Would Garima and Madhav want to celebrate with just three guests?"

I was disappointed when it came to the number of invites, but I couldn't do anything about it.

Two days later, it was finally my birthday! I woke up with excitement and was anticipating the start of my party the whole day. When afternoon came, the bell rang, and I was excited to find out who it was.

Just then, two Labrador dogs came into our house! Garima and Madhav brought them inside, and they had both come with some family members who dropped them off and then left. I felt very happy to see my special guests and I now understood why the guest list was so small: this party was for dogs only, just like me! I felt bad for making presumptions about Garima's invitation skills.

One of the dogs, Sam, had brought a decorated basket for my birthday gift. Madhav told me that the whole basket was all mine and my heart started jumping for joy! It looked so new and I could tell that it was full of food for me to eat! I thanked my friend a lot and got excited to see what the other one had brought for me, but it was very disappointing to find out that he had come empty-handed and his handler came with nothing for me. I felt very bad and was going to make a stink about it, but I thought that there was a chance that when his family came to pick him up and take him back home, they could bring a gift for me then, so I controlled my anger and didn't say anything to him.

Once the guests had arrived and were seated, Garima left the living room and came back holding a birthday cap for me. She put it on my head and I found it very uncomfortable. I tried to shake it off, but it just slid down the top of my head and hung off my chin. Madhav came up to me, adjusted the cap, and gave me some words of encouragement.

"Sultan, it's your special day. You have to look special and different from the other dogs. How will you look different if you don't have the hat on? Come on, keep the cap on for now."

What he said made sense, so I decided to keep the birthday cap on. I was waiting for the third guest, wondering why they hadn't come yet. I kept listening for the doorbell to ring, signalling the arrival of my third guest. My actual interest was the gift, I didn't care much for the guest but I couldn't wait to be gifted more food!

My guests were treated very well and served dog food. They were being treated so generously that it made me a little jealous. I felt like they were going to finish all of the food we had and then there would be nothing left for me to eat. It was relieving, then, to have some food served to me as well. Both of my guests were busy gobbling up their food and their speed was amazing to watch. It didn't even take them a minute to finish what had been served to them.

Sam had brought gift to me so I didn't mind it when he was served food, but I didn't like that Buzo was being shown the same generosity. Why should he get delicious food if he didn't even bring me anything? I ate my food and finished it no slower than my guests, and so I went back to playing with them and waiting for the third guest. Unfortunately, he never turned up.

When the party was over, everyone's family members came and took them back home. As they were leaving, Garima came up to me and told me that my third guest was Gabbar but he couldn't come.

"Gabbar has something called arthritis, and it makes it very difficult for him to move and he can't climb stairs. He couldn't come, but aunty has sent a gift for you."

Once I knew that I had gotten another gift, it lessened the disappointment of Buzo not getting a gift for me. Mom also gave me a surprise gift after our guests departed. Wow! There were two packets, one was full of toys and another had different types of biscuit packets, which were new to me. My heart started jumping out of joy. It had made my day!

My birthday party made me feel very important and special. I alone was the birthday boy, and it felt nice to have a day all about me. I thanked Garima and everyone else in the family for arranging my party, and I thanked my guests for coming and making it fun. I couldn't wait for my birthday next year!

I only wished that my birthday should come more often!

Chapter 47

Brut and His Sudden Demise

I knew another Labrador named Brut, and we would meet whenever Garima took me out for a walk. Over time, the both of us became good friends and we had become fond of each other. Brut used to go on walks with his helper while I was accompanied by Garima.

One day, as I was on a walk with Garima, we ran into Brut. I was surprised to see him because he looked very different. He was wearing a golden coat and a bowtie. "Why is he dressed so fancy?", I wondered.

I went near to greet him when his helper suddenly pulled him back and yelled at Garima to keep me away from him.

"His elder brother is getting married and Brut has to sit with the bridegroom in the ceremony. Please keep Sultan away, I can't have Brut's coat spoiled. Sultan can play with him tomorrow".

Garima had a hearty laugh and pulled me away from Brut. I thought it was funny that Brut's brother was the bridegroom when Brut was the one dressed up like he was getting married. When we went back home, Garima told Mom what had happened and Mom, too, had a laugh.

A few days later, when Garima had taken me for a walk again, we met Brut's helper. Brut, however, was not with him.

"How come you haven't brought Brut with you today? Where is he?", Garima asked him.

When the helper heard her ask that question, he started sobbing. Garima was clearly as shocked as I was, because she looked too nervous to say anything. After an uncomfortably long silence, Garima started to console him. My heart started beating faster because I was expecting some kind of terrible news from him.

After a few minutes, he composed himself and told us what had happened. "Brut has died." His eyes were filled with tears again and he couldn't say anything after that. Hearing what he said numbed me and Garima. She couldn't even think of what she should say on such an occasion. "I don't even think he was that old... was he?" "No, he wasn't", the helper replied.

"It happened suddenly", he continued. "We didn't understand anything about how it had happened. I have to leave now, Garima. I have a lot of work to do."

Garima nodded, and he left. We resumed our walk as well. While we were walking, I couldn't help but think about Brut. It was sad that he had died prematurely. I couldn't forget his face and his golden coat of hair. Can somebody just die so suddenly? Can it happen to anybody? Can it happen to me, too? I shuddered at the thought of it. We kept walking and eventually came home with heavy hearts.

After this incident, Garima took me and went to Brut's house to express her grief and condolences. She asked his aunty how it had happened.

"He was being given a bath by our helper. Maybe the water entered his nose or something, and he started choking. He was feeling uneasy because right after the bath, he went and sat under the bed."

Garima looked at her as she continued.

"We failed to understand the gravity of what was happening. I wish I had taken him to the doctor right away... If I had, he would have been alive today. Immediately after the bath, he sat under the bed and never got up. We thought he was hiding from us because he was reluctant to get dried with the towel. After some time, they told me he was hiding under the bed so I called out to him many times, but he never came out. It was then that we realized something was wrong. We pulled him out, but he was no longer alive. It was too late. We've buried him now. Sometimes I go there and sit with my lovely dog."

Garima sat there for some time and then we came back. She told Mom about it, who felt bad, too. I was now even more glad that Mom always bathed me herself. She has always been very careful when bathing me. Even when she takes the help of Meena or Mahinder, she never leaves me alone with them. When she's washing my head, she always raises it up so water never enters my nose, and she keeps my ears closed so no water gets in there, either. It was today that I realized just how important that was.

Chapter 48

Our New Air Conditioner

A few months later, Granny came to visit us. We were all sitting in the bedroom because it was really hot and only the bedrooms had air conditioners, there were none in the living room. Everyone ate lunch in their bedrooms instead of the living room. Mom and Granny were chatting as the kids were playing with me, and I was making sure to keep a safe distance away from Granny. She said she wanted one more cup of tea before leaving, and so we all went into the living room so she could have her tea on the table and not spill it on the bed. As she was slowly sipping her tea, the heat started to get to me and I put out my tongue so I could cool off. Mom asked me to go back to the cooler bedroom, but I liked everyone's company and conversations so I chose to stay.

"Sultan, I understand that you're happy here but it's too hot for you. Just go back to the bedroom, we'll be with you soon."

To my surprise, Granny interjected. "Do you really love him or are you saying all that just for show? Sultan is this, Sultan is that… look at how he's panting! He has no choice but to tolerate this heat to be in your company. Are you so poor that you can't even afford to install an air conditioner in the living room for your beloved Sultan!?"

Hearing this, the children chimed in and joined Granny in demanding a new A.C. be set up. Their tone was a bit complaining.

I was surprised to hear Granny say something so considerate. I wondered if I was seeing a change in Granny's attitude. Had I misjudged her after the whole slap thing? I had never seen her softer side. It was surprising to see her think so much of my comfort, and I felt a little bad for judging her solely off of one unpleasant happening. Her attitude was so impressive that I almost forgot about the slap episode altogether. Time passed, they had a few more conversations, and Granny left to go back home.

The next morning, Mom and Garima told Madhav that they were going to the market, but they didn't say what for. I found that very unusual because they always said why they were going somewhere before they left.

They came back home in the afternoon and a big box was delivered to our door a few hours later. When Madhav saw it, he asked Mom what it was.

"It's so big… what did you buy?"

"You don't need to ask me. Just read the label on the side."

Madhav read the label on the side of the box out aloud. "Hitachi… dual compressor… It's an A.C.!"

He went and hugged mom. It was nice to see him so excited!

I went near her, too, and started wagging my tail. Mom understood my feelings right away.

"Sultan, this is your gift. I know this room feels like a furnace to you. With this air conditioner installed, you won't be so uncomfortable here!"

Two people came in to install it, and they took a lot of time, Finally, once it was installed, one of them said that he wanted to give a demo about how to use the remote. Mom asked Madhav to learn it from them, and he switched on the A.C.

Cool air! It felt like getting out of a pool and feeling a nice breeze blow on you. The entire living room soon went from hot to cool. Mom thanked the installation worker and paid them for their work, and then they left. We were all overjoyed to see the living room be so comfortable now. We spent some time relaxing, and eventually, Papa came back home from the office.

When he came in, he didn't seem pleased to see the new A.C.

"Why is there an A.C. here? Who bought it? What even was the need to put this here? There are already two A.C.s in the two bedrooms. It's really sad that no one even thought to tell me about such a big decision."

Mom told him everything that had happened and told him what Granny had said, but he didn't seem convinced.

"We can't install a third one", he said. "Our colony only allows two per household."

Mom gave him a smart reply, "We will only use two at a time. The third one will always be off. See, this is why I didn't tell you about it. I knew that your answer would always be a no, no matter what. Look how happy Garima and Madhav are that this is here. Look how much more comfortable Sultan is!"

Both the kids were surprised, saying that they had been asking for another air conditioner for a whole three years, and she only decided to get one when Granny made it about me.

"Are we your real children? Or do you love Sultan more than us?", they asked with great concern.

I was surprised to hear this and I, too, wondered why she hadn't bought this A.C. earlier. At the same time, it made me realize just how important I was for the entire family. Mom told the kids that she just couldn't afford to buy this thing until now, and apologized to the kids.

They said that they were just teasing her and that they were just happy that it finally got installed.

"Now we can study in this room! Mom, we're glad that you took an independent decision and ignored the colony's stupid rules. We will make best use of this room," said Garima. You have turned the room from an arid desert to a cool mountain peak."

Mom seemed relieved to hear that and thanked them for forgiving her so easily.

Madhav then asked Mom how much she had paid for it, saying that it seemed pretty expensive because of the "dual compressor".

"Forty-five thousand", she replied.

He seemed shocked, saying that it was very expensive and that he was surprised that she would spend so much money for my comfort. I thanked Granny for making this happen. Even though I didn't know how much money that was, I knew that it was a lot.

The living room became a very pleasant place to relax. Mom started watching the TV more. Garima and Madhav started sitting at the dining table to study. Even Papa became happy that the A.C. was cooling as well as it was because the study room that he spent a lot of time in was right in front of the living room, and the cold air would make its way into his room as well. Madhav would often say that Mummy had turned the room from an arid desert to a cool mountain peak. I had never been to those places, but I knew that it meant that the room was now very nice to be in.

I felt very lucky to have such a caring and considerate family, and to have a Granny that cared so much for my comfort. Installation of the A.C., showed me how important I was to Mom and that she really meant it when she called me her third child. It felt like my family never discriminated against me because I was a dog!

Chapter 49

A Mishappening

One day, a very hilarious incident took place. Mom was sitting at the dining table, probably preparing something for her school. Our television was kept on a shelf built into the wall, and its wires hung outside the shelf. Madhav and I were playing with each other, and he was chasing me when I ran past the wires. He kept chasing me, not knowing that his leg was pulling on the wires, and soon a loud sound startled us, what had happened and both of us were shocked to see our beloved television lying face-down on the floor.

We were both scared, I think because both of us expected to be punished. I stood still like a statue, expecting a thrashing from Mom. I looked at her to see her reaction, and she was holding her head in her hands in disbelief.

"*Meena!*", she yelled out, calling to him.

"Come and see if our TV is still alive or dead!", she told him.

I had no hopes of the TV still being alive and fine. Meena walked into the scene, lifted up the TV, and put it back on the shelf, putting all the wires where they belonged. I was quite surprised to see that the screen and frame were completely fine. Only the base had gotten cracked.

I turned around to look at Mom again and saw her thanking God for saving our TV. Madhav felt very sorry for what he had done and kept apologizing to Mom. She told him that it wasn't his fault, that I was the one who had pulled the wires but that we should both have taken care. Madhav was very innocent so he believed what she said, but I knew the truth and got very angry at the false accusation.

When Papa came home in the evening, Mom narrated the whole thing to him, how Madhav was chasing me and how my legs got entangled in the wires and pulled the television down. I was surprised to hear her blame me for it once again, it made me confused and a little angry. Papa asked her about the condition of the TV, and she showed him that it was fine and functioning well.

"Oh, thank god...", Papa said as he breathed a sigh of relief and looked at me.

"Sultan, play more carefully in the future."

After saying that to me, he left to change out of his uniform. I got even angrier because I was now being blamed for something that was Madhav's fault!

Later, Garima came home from college and Mom told her about what had happened, too, but this time she didn't blame me and took Madhav's name instead. She also told her that she had told Madhav and Papa that it was Sultan's fault. Garima asked her why she blamed me when it wasn't my fault, which was just what I had been wondering this whole time.

"If I had told your Papa it was Madhav's fault, he might have scolded him, but I know that your Papa would never scold Sultan. Besides, Madhav was already feeling very guilty so I tried to make him believe that he wasn't the one at fault."

Garima agreed with Mom and told her that she had done the right thing.

"That's true. Papa would probably have scolded Madhav."

When I heard Mom's explanation, my anger evaporated in seconds. I wasn't mad at Madhav anymore, and I felt satisfied knowing that I had saved him from being scolded and feeling guilty all day. Mom's decision really showed her wisdom!

Chapter 50

Fleas and their Havoc

Several months later, Garima had taken admission in a college, from which she used to return in the evening. She never forgot to talk to me first and then she would eat something. Then she used to play with me, which I always liked very much. One day, we started playing as usual but I was not able to continue playing for longer. I sat in one corner and started itching because I was feeling sharp pricks all over my body. Garima tried to boost my morale to continue playing but I couldn't help the itching. She couldn't understand anything so she went to Mom and said, "Mom, Sultan is always eager to play but now I'm noticing a big change in his behaviour. He isn't able to play and keeps itching. Is he suffering from some infection? I think that we need to immediately consult a doctor for him."

Mom assured her that she would do everything she could to help me and from that point onwards, she started watching me closely. By now, Papa had also noticed that I had started itching a lot so he too asked Mom to show me to the doctor. The next day, Mom and Meena took me to the vet. When we arrived at the clinic, Mom wished the doctor a good morning and asked him to give me a checkup after telling him about my itching and how they had no idea why it had gotten so bad. The doctor assured her that he would check me very patiently. He then started examining my skin and concluded that I was suffering from some kind of skin infection.

He prescribed me some medicines and a lotion to be applied on my skin. After Meena went and purchased the medicines, we got in the car and left to go back home. As soon as we had reached our house, Mom asked Meena to wash his hands and apply the lotion on my skin. I was given the tablets in my food right after and so began my treatment.

Even though my treatment had started, it was not giving me any relief from the itching. Mom also noticed that I was not responding to the medication. Then, as is usual for our last resort, Bhanwar Singh was called to check on me and solve my problem. The next day, he came to our house and Mom told him about my problem and the treatment that wasn't working for me. Bhanwar Singh assured my family very confidently that he would do his best to get me rid of my itching and whatever problem I had. He then started grooming me vigorously and kept at it for quite some time. When he was through I sat down peacefully because my itching had finally gone away. After looking at how comfortable I finally was, he had a proud look on his face and as usual he got a lot of appreciation and gratitude from my Papa and Mom.

A few minutes later, Bhanwar Singh said that he had to leave. Mom asked him to have tea and some snacks but he politely refused. Some time after he left, however, I started feeling sharp pricks all over my body again, just as before. When Mom saw this, she said to Papa, "I think that Bhanwar Singh has failed to detect his problem for the first time. I just can't figure out why no one is able to diagnose him properly... we're ignorant because we have no previous experience of keeping a dog but his suffering is increasing day by day. I don't know what to do..." Papa tried to console her but to no avail.

The next day in the morning, when I was sitting in the balcony with Mom, she lovingly said to me, "My Dear Sultan, what has happened to you? Why is no one able to make out anything, not even Bhanwar Singh?" Then she started giving me a gentle massage on my head. Suddenly the tone of her voice changed and she said, "Oh my god. What the hell? So this is the evil causing my son so much trouble!" She immediately yelled for Meena to bring some hot water while keeping her hand on my forehead. She had noticed that some little bugs were gathering around my eyes, which she started picking up and Meena started killing. They must have killed more than sixty of the things in just about half an hour. She was shocked to see so many of them in just a small area, so she went back inside the house and told Papa about them, calling them "fleas". He advised her to take me to some other hospital and she immediately took an appointment from the Veterinary Hospital.

On the assigned day I was taken to the hospital, she told the doctor that she had seen fleas on my body. The doctor asked the compounder to comb my hair, and when he did he found a flea in the very first stroke. After he showed it to the doctor, the doctor was fully convinced that I had fleas. He gave me an injection for something and then sprayed my whole body with a medicine. The compounder closed my mouth with a bandage and told me it was so I wouldn't lick my body. The doctor then asked Meena to take me for a walk out in the open for about fifteen minutes. Mom asked the doctor whether the spray was effective or not and he assured that it was very effective for getting rid of fleas. This made Mom confident that I would be flea-free now and my problems would come to an end. To be completely sure, she also bought a comb and later told Meena that they would use it on me every day to check if I still had fleas.

The morning after, when Mom started combing me with the flea comb, she almost fainted when she saw the number of fleas caught in the comb again! She immediately told Meena to bring hot water in a mug, which he brought hurriedly. Mom put all the fleas in the hot water to kill them. She must have combed me for half an hour and in every stroke, she was catching more fleas. Meena was making sure that fleas didn't come out of the mug alive. Both of them were hoping that they could bring an end to the fleas on my body. They did the same thing the next day and fleas were still getting trapped in the comb, with Meena picking them up and putting them in hot water. This must have continued for around ten days or so. Mom got tired of this routine and she was very worried that I was infested with fleas.

Finally, she called Bhanwar Singh to consult him about my problem once again. He came to our house and after looking around he said, "Maybe your furniture has become infested with fleas. Even if you kill all of the ones on Sultan, more will appear the next day. They take shelter in wooden furniture so I would suggest that the entire house be sprayed with a chemical. It is slightly poisonous, but it will definitely solve your problem. You need to dilute it in water, then mop the entire house with that chemical. When the staff is mopping and spraying, no other person should be there in the house. Once they are done, they should then close all the windows and doors. Meena should open the house and all the windows back up after half an hour. The rest of the family can enter the house afterwards."

The next day, Meena went to the market and brought the chemical Bhanwar Singh talked about. While he was diluting the chemical, he asked us to leave and come back to the house about forty-five minutes later. All of us did exactly like Bhanwar Singh had asked us to do. We went to Mrs. Lalchand's house to spend our time. When it was safe for us to go back to our home, Meena came to us and said that we could safely enter the house. Mrs. Lalchand appreciated Meena for completing this hazardous work, to which he politely replied, "I can do anything for Sultan, this was just a chemical." Then Mom expressed her desire to leave and we headed for home. Though we had entered the house after a safe time, I could still smell the chemical fumes around us.

The next day, Mom triumphantly exclaimed, "Now we've finally gotten rid of these bloodsuckers, thanks to Bhanwar Singh. Meena, come here with a mug and hot water, let's see if we succeeded."

She confidently started combing me. To her disappointment, she caught fleas in the very first stroke of the comb! Horrified to see them again, she could do anything but hold her head in her hands. Alas!

Chapter 51

Fleas and Their End

Now all my family members were really very worried. All of them were discussing what was to be done. Papa asked Mom, "Neelam, what are you planning to do now? We've tried everything to no avail. These bloody fleas are infinite in number. We have to do something, the matter is very serious."

Mom said that it indeed was a very serious matter and she asked for some time to think about how to go about getting rid of the fleas.

Suddenly Madhav gave a pleasant surprise to the family with a suggestion. "We've tried everything but failed miserably. I think we should hit this at the root cause. The fleas are hiding in his thick black hair, so we should think of giving him a haircut! If there's no hair, where will the fleas hide?" Papa exclaimed, "Madhav, you always think outside the box! We could have never thought of this, it's a brilliant idea." Everyone liked the idea very much and everyone thanked Madhav for it. Garima teased him, saying, "Madhav, now you've proven by giving a useful idea that There's still some stuff left in your head." Everyone started laughing but I didn't like this joke because I was not at all in favour of getting a haircut. I shuddered to imagine a bald Sultan. I wanted to say no to this idea but no one had even taken my consent!

The next day, I was sent with Meena for my haircut with Bhanwar Singh joining us mid-way. I was being taken to a veterinary clinic in Ashok Vihar. Bhanwar Singh took me to the doctor and told him about my problem. He told the doctor that my family had tried everything but the result was so poor that they had now sent me for a haircut. The doctor called two compounders and instructed them to cut my hair. They took me and asked Meena to pick me up and put me on a table nearby, which he did gently. In the meantime, the compounders brought their tools over and started cutting my hair. I felt terrible knowing I would be bald but I was helpless... when they were cutting my hair, everyone was surprised to see the number of fleas! One compounder started picking up my hair and started burning it so that the fleas couldn't escape and jump onto some other dogs there.

Bhanwar Singh said to Meena, "Meena, I wonder how Sultan was living with so many fleas on his body. Bloody fleas have made him wounded. Look at his back and how patchy it's become. I think they have made him anemic, Poor chap! It was clearly a very good decision to send him for the haircut. Initially, I didn't agree with the decision but I couldn't say no to Sir. I thought that the fipronil medication would prove effective, but now I see that this haircut was the only way to get rid of the fleas."

After getting my haircut, I was taken for a bath. Once it was over, Bhanwar Singh took me back to the doctor. The doctor said that the fleas had made my condition miserable. He gave a lotion for my wounds and said that the lotion would heal them and have a soothing effect. After that, we went back to our car and left for home.

I was sitting in the car and thinking about my sorry condition and that I had surely become bald now. I thought, "I must look very ugly without my shiny black hair. Why did my family take such a cruel decision without my consent? How will I enter my house? Will my family members accept me even with how ugly I must look?"

I was sure no one would like me anymore. If only I could run out of the car!

There were so many questions and apprehensions in my mind. I was afraid that my family would disown me for my repulsive looks. Suddenly, the driver applied the brakes. I thought that we had reached our colony but I saw only Bhanwar Singh getting out of the car. Before leaving, he looked back at me and said, "Sultan, it's good that you were sent for getting a haircut. I could never have imagined that you were infested with so many fleas. This could be dangerous for your life, you know! It can be fatal for a dog's life if fleas or ticks remain on the body for a long time. I'm very happy now with your family's decision and I can see that it was a wise idea."

Perhaps the focus of my thought process started changing then. After listening to Bhanwar Singh's words, I started thinking about what was more important for me: my looks, or my life. Now I was confused and didn't know what to think.

The driver started the car again. After some time, we reached our colony and my heart started beating faster. I was hesitant to enter the house but I knew that there was no avoiding it. I entered the house and ran in very fast to hide myself under the bed. I kept sitting under the bed for the whole day and only came out in the evening to eat something. To my surprise, I saw that no one disliked me without my coat of hair. Rather, everyone was eagerly waiting for me to come out. I felt more confident now so I went out for my evening walk without any hesitation. Even now, I was feeling very itchy and could still feel some pricks, though there was some relief.

When I came back from my walk, my family saw me closely. They saw the marks of the flea bites and everyone empathised with me. Madhav said, "The fleas have played havoc with Sultan. We couldn't understand his suffering; the biting marks show just how much he has suffered. We were thinking that he has some allergy towards something but the actual problem was altogether different." He continued, "Mumma, it was a good idea to send him for his haircut. His torture would have continued if you had not noticed the fleas yesterday. Congratulations to all of us, there is not a single flea on his body now."

I also congratulated myself for getting rid of the blood sucking fleas. I also felt better as the itching had reduced to some extent. Papa said to me, "My sweetheart, my child, there is no need to feel ashamed of yourself. Good looking or bad looking, you are ours now. I must say, though, that comfort is more important than mere looks. Soon you will have see hair growth again because you are still young. You don't have to worry about it."

I felt better after listening to this. I wrongly thought that I had now become bald and ugly forever. Now I had also changed my mind about haircuts. I realized that my family had taken the right decision because they had tried everything else but failed miserably. Remembering the sharp needle-like prickes changed my opinion completely. I remembered Bhanwar Singh's words, that tick fever could be fatal for me. I was also compelled to think that life was definitely more important than looks. Now I started thanking my family for having made such a wise decision.

Chapter 52

A Compassionate Family

I was in the car with Mom as she was on her way to school, with Meena sitting in the front next to the driver. Out of the window, she saw a dog with no hair. His whole body was covered in red patches and he looked very itchy.

"Meena, did you see that dog?", she asked him as the car moved by.

He said that he had indeed seen the dog and that he felt very bad for him because he had lost all of his hair and was miserably itchy.

Mom promised Meena that she would do something about the dog when she came back from school. When she came back home after her day at school was over, she rang up an animal care hospital on the phone and asked them what could be done to help the poor dog she saw earlier. I didn't hear their response, but she looked disappointed to hear it. She then called Bhanwar Singh and I could tell that he had told her to use some kind of medicine and give it to the dog twice a day.

She then called out to Meena and asked him to buy a pack of "Neomac". He left to buy it and when he came back with it, Mom asked him to give it to the dog they saw twice a day for seven days.

Meena started doing so religiously, feeding the dog the medicine with milk and bread so it would eat it. I think he did his duty very well because the dog started to look better after just two days! It was a very pleasant surprise for all of us.

I was very happy with the approach my family took and how empathetic they had shown themselves to be. Mom asked Meena and Mahinder to buy some more medicine and treat other dogs with it if they found any.

One morning, as he was leaving to drive Papa to the office, Pawan told Mom that he had seen a wounded eagle on his drive back home the previous night. She advised that he pick it up and take it to a bird hospital. When he told her that he was too scared to go near it, she told him to call a Jain Animal Care Centre and tell them about it. That evening, when Papa came back from the office and Pawan came to drop off his briefcase, he told Mom that the centre had called him to tell him that they had successfully rescued the eagle, much to Mom's relief.

A few days later, as she was taking me for my routine car ride in the colony, she saw a dog drinking dirty water from a bucket that a boy was using to clean a car. She asked Mahinder to put some clay bowls down there and fill them with clean water every day so the dogs wouldn't have to drink dirty water. Mahinder took some money from her and went and bought the bowls as she had asked. He put them in a few different places, and when he came back inside, Meena told Mom that he had done his job well. Mom appreciated his work and expressed her gratitude.

When we left for our evening walk, Mom tried to look for the bowls of water, but couldn't find any of them. She spoke to Mahinder immediately, and he said that he was certain he had put them down himself. It was then that Meena spoke up, saying that they had probably been picked up and stolen by people.

"They wouldn't even spare bowls meant for dogs," he said.

Mom was angry to think that was the case.

"How cheap! This kind of behaviour is disgusting. I'm not just going to sit down and let this happen, Meena. I'm going to do something about this."

Hearing how upset Mummy was that some dogs whom she didn't even know were deprived of clean water showed me yet again how sensitive and caring my family and our helpers were. I admired how they approached situations with empathy. If only all humans thought like them, no animal would suffer like that dog or the eagle. After that incident, Mom made such arrangement for dogs that hardly anyone would like to steal, telling Mahinder to put down old, cracked and barely usable pots instead of new ones. Mahinder used to fill those slightly broken pots with clean water for the dogs.

God has made people much more capable of helping living things than a dog like myself, so I felt like it was their responsibility to help the animals that are suffering. I felt happy that my family was fulfilling its duties well.

Chapter 53

A Wild Life Case

One day, I heard Garima said to Mom, "Mummy, are we going the market? Should I get ready?" Mom angrily replied, "Garima, I had told you yesterday that we have to go the market with Mrs. Lalchand and her daughter for their shopping. Now I am ready to leave and you are asking me this again." Garima replied that she will just take a minute to get ready. She again said to Mom, "I think that we are taking two cars. I have to sit with you but I would prefer sitting in Mrs. Lalchand's car, is it okay with you?" Mom replied, "First you get ready. And I don't have any problem if you sit with Divya and her Mom. Why would I object to your choice?"

Garima went to a room and got ready for the market while Mom was waiting for her in the living room. When Garima came, she asked Mom, "Mummy, will we eat something? I am feeling very hungry." Mom replied, "Garima, we just have to show them the boutique and then we will come back. Let's not delay anymore and get a move on." Both of them said bye to me and left for the market. I started wagging my tail in approval.

It was my lunchtime so I took my food and went out for my walk with Mahinder. I was hoping that by the time I would be back I would definitely see both Mom and Garima. I came back from the walk but didn't find them in the entire house. I thought, "It was their lunchtime and Garima must be feeling very hungry by now. Why they have not come back yet?" I tried waiting for them but I started feeling drowsy and soon I fell asleep. I woke up after a few hours but found that Mom and Garima had not reached back. I wondered, they were supposed to be back by lunchtime and it was evening now. I was desperately waiting for them. Fnally, the doorbell rang and I ran towards the door.

Meena went and opened the door and I felt very happy to see both Garima and Mom. I noticed that Garima was holding a very small puppy and she had an apologetic look on her face. When they entered the room, Mom angrily asked her, "Now tell me your stupid story, I want to know everything." I was surprised that Garima had brought a puppy, I was very sure that my family was not going to replace me with it.... but then why?

Soon Garima started telling Mom, "Mummy, I was sitting with Divya in the car, and the car had stopped at a red signal. Then a man came, he was very drunk and was holding this puppy by the skin of its neck. He said that he was ready to sell this Labrador puppy for three thousand rupees. I just wanted to save this puppy from that drunkard so I bargained hard and brought him down to three hundred rupees. I just wanted to save the puppy, nothing more."

Mom said to her, "Tell me the exact place where that man was standing. You couldn't save its life but I definitely will. Wait a minute Garima, I think I have also seen that man, he had come near my car also but I refused. He was badly drunk, a tall and sturdy fellow. I saw him near Haldi Ram's shop. Am I right?" Garima exclaimed and said, "Yes, Mom. You are right." Meena was standing there like a silent spectator with a curious expression on his face. Mom lovingly picked up the puppy and went to the balcony as I followed her. She put the puppy down, maybe wanting it to pee but it didn't. I started smelling the puppy which made me feel nostalgic about my early childhood, about the day when I had joined my family. Mom waited for some time and brought the puppy in, and I followed her back into the house. She was looking very upset at this development so she asked Garima again, "Give me one solid reason why you bought this puppy."

She almost weepingly replied, "I thought that we could keep this puppy with us for some days and look for a family that could take him. When we found one, we would give the puppy away." Mom took a long breath and asked Meena to bring an empty box and a few old clothes. Meena immediately brought both the things within a few minutes. Then Mom told Meena, "I am going to Karol Bagh Police Station to catch hold of that fraud man, I am sure he will be back on the streets selling puppies again soon. Meena, just give me a glass of water, I have not taken water since afternoon. Then she said to the children, "Tell your Papa that I am going to the police station and will try to come back soon."

When Garima heard this, she offered to accompany Mom but she denied. Madhav who was listening to everything intently, said, "Garima, that is not the right place for you to visit. I am confident that Mumma will set everything right. She will definitely get that cruel man punished." In the meantime, Meena spread the clothes out in the small box and then carefully kept the puppy in it. Mom picked up the carton and went downstairs.

Meena said to Garima, "Didi, he has cheated you. It was a street dog, not a Labrador. He has played with your emotions and made fool out of you." I looked at her and saw that she had a sorry look on her face. After some time, Papa came home from the office. He saw that Garima was sitting in the living room and was looking very upset. Papa asked her, "Garima, why you are looking so worried? Is everything alright?" She initially hesitated to share her problem but after a few minutes she narrated the entire episode to Papa.

When he heard this, he started laughing and said, "You are an expert in creating some issue or the other. Where is your mummy?" Before Garima could say anything Madhav replied in a rebellious tone, "Papa, she hasn't created any issue, and if at all she has then Mumma has gone to the Karol Bagh Police Station to set things right." I think Papa was not in a mood to confront him so he quietly left the living-room. Madhav consoled Garima and said, "Don't worry. You have not done anything wrong. Besides, I am sure that Mom will come with some good news." All of us started waiting for Mom in suspense.

After a long wait, the doorbell rang and we ran towards the door. Meena opened the door to mom eho was standing outside. She came in, looking relieved but quite tired. Both the children started asking from her about the matter. She said, "Give me some water to drink first. I am feeling very thirsty." Garima rushed to the kitchen and brought water for Mom.

When Mom had finished the water, she took a deep breath, in the meantime Papa had also entered the living room. He said to Mom, "I am happy that you are back, but do you that know it is 9 P.M.? Why you are so late?" Mom said,

"I went to the police station with the puppy. One constable was sitting there, I narrated the entire episode to him. He asked me if I wanted my money back but I refused. Then he asked me "Madam, what do you want, if not your money?" I told him clearly, "I have not come here all the way from Connaught Place for a measly three hundred rupees. I request you to kindly reunite the puppy with his mother because he is too young to survive without his mother's milk. That man has separated a newborn from his mother. Is this not a crime?" The constable smiled and said, "I really appreciate your kind attitude for animals but how will we trace that man? He must have disappeared by now."

Mom said, "I had taken the same route coming here and saw that man still selling another newborn." The constable immediately got up and took me to the Inspector's room. Then he introduced me to the inspector and said, "Sir, today a wildlife case has come before us." After the constable explained everything to him, the inspector was surprised and looked at me. I told him, "I don't want my money back, I just want this newborn to be reunited with his mother. When I was coming to the police station I saw the man and he was still selling another little puppy. I think that this is a crime against the mother and her babies. He needs to be stopped and punished." The inspector seemed happy to hear this, shared a plan with the constable and asked him to get into action.

Mom was asked to use our car to reach there, the cops had to sit in their van. She was asked to get down from the car and try to recognise him to see if he was the same person she had seen earlier and to give a signal to the van if he was. She continued, "When I reached the same place, I got down from the car and recognised the man. To my luck, he was still doing that nasty work.

After recognising him, I gave a signal to the van. The cops got down and caught him red-handed. He was taken into the van, meanwhile a huge crowd had gathered there to witness the scene. Some people knew that I had given a signal to the van so they asked me what the matter was. I told them in brief that man was separating newborn puppies from their mother and I was just trying to stop this. You know, they even congratulated me for doing such a wonderful thing. They also said that I had inspired them to take such corrective measures themselves."

She continued. "After we left and reached the police station, I was asked to sit in one room. That man was brought to the room and was dealt with strictly. He confessed that he had been doing this for a long time. He promised everyone that he would never do this in future. The cops told him to accompany them to reunite both the puppies with their mother. He readily agreed and then the constable told me that I could leave now. He promised me that he would personally see to it that the babies were reunited with their mother"

Everybody present in the room gave a big round of applause to mom. Garima and Madhav gave her a big hug. When I saw them hugging her, I also jumped onto the sofa and started licking her hand while wagging my tail. She said, "I know, all my children are very happy to know that two puppies have been reunited with their mother." Papa also congratulated mom for being a brave heart, he also said that she could have taken his help. She said that she did not want to bother him. Madhav then raised his voice out loud, "Three cheers for Delhi Police!"

"Hip-hip hurray,!" Garima and Madhav shouted together. I also joined the chorus with my joyful bow-bow!

Chapter 54

A Walk in Lodhi Garden

One day, Garima told Mom about a place called Lodhi Garden, saying that it was a nice place to go for a walk and that dogs were allowed inside. Mom was very happy to hear that I, too, could go for a walk to the same place as her.

"We're going to stop going to the Railway Stadium, then. I want Sultan to come with us so I can see to it that he has fun and becomes physically fit."

And so it was decided that I, Madhav, Garima, and Mummy would all go for our evening walk to Lodhi garden. It was a little far from our house, so I was very excited to discover a new place. It was boring for me to just sit at home whenever Mom and Garima went to the Railway Stadium for their walks.

That evening, we left for Lodhi garden in our car. Satyendra was driving us there and we were accompanied by Meena, who would walk me and take care of me. After driving for about half an hour, we finally reached the garden. Satyendra stopped the car and everyone got out one-by-one. Meena was holding my leash and the two of us got out of the car as well. However, no one was aware that some street dogs had smelled me and started coming towards me. Meena immediately scared them away with a bamboo stick he had, but I still felt scared. Satyendra and Meena guarded me and escorted me into the garden.

When we had arrived, Mom asked Meena to meet her at the entrance after forty-five minutes, saying that they would all meet up at the same spot that they came in from. She also said that the garden was very big and it would be difficult for them to catch up to each other, so they would stay in touch using their mobile phones. I wished I had a phone of my own! As I looked around, I felt amazed to be in such a huge, vast and open space, full of trees everywhere.

Everyone split up, with Meena and Satyendra taking me for a walk in one direction and my family members going in the other direction for their walk. Meena and Satyendra took me to a big open lawn and started running around with me, which was very fun! We played games together and time passed by quickly. Soon, it was time to meet up at the entrance, so we left and reunited with Mom and the others.

Mom saw that I was panting because of how hot it was, and she asked Meena to give me some cold water. I was surprised to see that my family had come fully prepared, and I was actually given water that had ice in it to keep it cold. I sated my thirst and felt much better, and then we left to go back home.

Once we had arrived, Satyendra handed the car keys over to Meena after parking it and we all walked into the elevator. When we were back at home, I was surprised to see that my dinner was already prepared. Mahinder had prepared my dinner before I had even left for Lodhi Garden. How considerate!

I gulped down my food and quickly went to sleep. It hadn't dawned on me that I was very tired from running around so much. I had never run so much in my life! Meena tried moving me to make me get up so I could go on my evening walk, but I didn't want to move. Garima then tried to convince me to get up.

"I know you're tired, but you need to go for a walk after having a big meal. That wasn't a snack, it was a proper dinner. You need to go for a walk after eating it. If you're so tired from being in Lodhi Garden, we won't take you there again."

I definitely didn't want to miss going to Lodhi Garden again, so I got up and left with Meena for my evening walk.

When I came back, I was feeling even more tired than before. Madhav had already turned the A.C on and my bed was already laid. I thanked him in my heart, sat on my mattress and soon fell asleep. It was very relaxing to finally be in bed after such a long day.

I woke up in the morning to the sounds of chanting and prayer. It was definitely Mom doing her morning routine out on the balcony, so I ran out to be with her. Her eyes were closed and she was fully focused on performing her breathing exercises. I patiently waited for a few minutes, but when she paid no attention to me I started whining. It worked, and she slowly opened her eyes to look at me.

"I didn't wake you up because I knew how hectic yesterday was for you. I was just waiting. Come here..."

She took me on her lap and resumed her exercise. I was content.

Everyone started their day as they usually did, but it was different for me. I eagerly awaited the evening. Whenever my family members wanted to measure time, they would look at the wall clock. Whenever I did it, however, I didn't understand anything. I didn't know how much time was left until sunset, so time passed by very slowly for me. I felt so impatient that I couldn't even sleep properly in the afternoon.

By that time, everyone had started to come back home. Mummy came home first, then Madhav, and finally Garima. I understood that we would soon leave to go to Lodhi Garden. Garima asked Meena to pack my bag and everyone changed into sportswear. When everyone was ready, we locked the doors and left. Just like before, there were many street dogs at the entrance, but when they saw the stick in Meena's hand they kept their distance. We had safely arrived at Lodhi Garden.

Mom once again told Satyendra to meet up after forty-five minutes. Today, I was taken to a different lawn, one that was very big. We played a lot, and I enjoyed running around freely with no leash on my body. I didn't bother any person nearby because I only cared about playing with Satyendra and Meena. We played so much that we got tired quickly and had to sit down for a break, but once we regained our strength we got back up and started playing again. Meena then surprised me with a ball that he had kept in my bag.

"Sultan, let's play a new game this time. I'll throw this ball, and we'll see who can get it and bring it back to me first: you or Satyendra."

He then threw the ball and I ran towards it as fast as I could. Satyendra couldn't run faster than me, so I got the ball and brought it back first.

"Sultan wins! Satyendra loses!", Meena exclaimed.

"Sultan... you run... really fast," Satyendra said as he paused to catch his breath.

"I had thought... you're just a child... so I could easily... outrun... you..."

I was so much faster than him that he still hadn't caught his breath! It felt great to be so quick. Afterwards, Meena asked us to pack up and go meet Mom. I hadn't realized that our time was already up. When we reached the meeting point, we saw Mom and the kids already waiting for us. Before Mom could say something, Satyendra apologized to her and said that they had gotten so carried away with playing games that they had lost track of time.

"Don't worry, we just got here. We haven't been waiting for long."

We then walked towards the exit and our car. Meena gave me water to drink, and then everyone got inside to go home.

Going to the garden became a daily routine for us. We would go together and then split up. Mom would tell everyone to meet up at the same point sometime later. Meena would then take me somewhere and we would play and have fun. One day, Satyendra asked Meena if he was bored.

"The three of us do the same thing every day. Let's change it up and explore the garden."

Meena agreed with him and we started walking. After walking for a bit, we had arrived at a bridge that stood over a pond. Satyendra pointed out some ducks to me.

"Sultan, do you see that? The swimming birds are called ducks."

The pond was really big. It was so big that the longer I looked at it, the bigger it seemed to be. And the ducks! They looked like bigger chickens. The ducks swam very gracefully. It almost looked like they were rhythmically dancing on the water with the way that they would swim and then suddenly change direction.

I thought about how the entire group of ducks was able to coordinate their actions. Were they somehow communicating? Whichever direction they went in, they went together. I could have spent the entire evening looking at the ducks, but Meena asked me to move.

"I know you like this pond and the ducks, but we have to go back to the entrance. Madam must be waiting for us, and if we spend too much time here we will be late."

And so we left and went home. I kept thinking about the ducks on our ride back.

Chapter 55

I Became a Villain in Lodhi Garden

Lodhi Garden was very big and very lush. Whenever we went, we could see people of all ages doing all kinds of exercises. Some would be walking, some would be jogging and some would play games. I had hardly seen anyone sitting idle.

Many children would play cricket and football on the big lawns. Every part of the park seemed to have people in it, and it was difficult to find a spot with no one there.

One day, when we were going back home, a beggar came up to our car at a traffic light. She started knocking on the car windows, but no one would open any. The woman, however, was very stubborn and kept banging on the window desperately. Everyone was getting irritated because of the unwanted noise. We started at the green signal and she turned back with a disappointed look on her face. We eventually reached our colony and got home.

All of us used to enjoy spending time at Lodhi Garden but the beggar had become a fun spoiler. She would appear and start banging at our window whenever our car would stop at the signal. It would irritate everyone, but nobody could do anything to stop it.

One day, the beggar came up to our car again and started knocking on the window as usual. I found out then that she had never noticed my presence before. When she knocked again very authoritatively, Mom opened the window and I greeted her with a loud bark. She got terrified and ran away for fear of her life! It was a very funny scene and everyone started laughing. Satyendra praised me and said that I had done a great job, that the beggar would never come close to our car again. My heart filled with pride as everyone thanked me for getting rid of an unwanted beggar. Satyendra turned out to be right because the woman never came near our car again. Yay!

Our routine of taking evening walks continued for many months. By now, I had explored the entire garden except for one stretch that Meena never allowed me to go into. It was like a patch of forest. There were many tall trees that people would rest under. One day, when the three of us were playing with a ball, it accidentally fell near one of those trees. It was my turn to bring the ball back, so I started running in the same direction that it flew.

Suddenly, I heard Meena's voice reach out me, "Sultan, stop! Don't go that way!"

I stopped, but I was quite close to the small forest. I saw that the people there were young girls and boys, sitting close to each other. They were doing something strange and trying to hide themselves from other people, which made me want to know what they were doing even more. Before I could go closer and get a better look, Meena came up to me and pulled me away, saying that the woods were not the right place for me. I walked back with him reluctantly, but even after we started playing again my attention stayed on the tall trees and the people there.

My curiosity grew day by day but I could never find out what they were doing because Meena would never allow me to go near them. I wanted to see them up close, I wanted to know more about their mysterious activities. The more Meena tried to stop me from going there, the more I wanted to go. I wanted to come up with some kind of plan, but I couldn't think of anything.

"Will I never find out what those people do in the dark?", thought I.

I didn't have the answers to any of my questions.

One day, when we were in the car on our way to Lodhi Garden, Mom told Meena that her group would take me for my walk, saying that it would make for a nice change.

"Mummy, if we take Sultan with us then we will be disturbing the other walkers. I don't think we should," Garima said.

"We'll walk on the grass, not the pavement. We won't be in the way of any of the walkers or joggers."

Garima liked the idea and I felt very happy to have the chance to walk with my family members today. When we arrived, Mom told Satyendra that since I was going with her, he could spend the forty-five minutes we had doing whatever he wanted and told him to relax.

We left for our walk, and as we approached the tall trees Mummy made an enlightening comment.

"Look over there", she said with a chuckle. "Those brothers and sisters sitting under the trees. They're having a good time."

She started laughing, and Garima asked her to show some self-control. I didn't know what she meant, but I now knew that the boys and girls there were brothers and sisters. I still didn't know what it is that they were doing, but it felt great to have part of the mystery finally solved.

"You're certainly an expert when it comes to spotting these 'brothers' and 'sisters'. Did you come here for the walk or just to watch a scene?"

I didn't like the comment Garima had just made. If Mom was an expert in solving mysteries and spotting those shady people then she deserved to be praised for it, not criticized. I was then surprised to see that we were walking on the path leading up to the tall trees. Mom was taking me in the same direction as the brothers and sisters, where Meena had never let me go.

I wanted to get closer to them and see what they were doing with each other, but Mom held me back with my leash, stopping me from getting close. When we got near a brother and sister, Mom tripped on something and loosened her grip on my leash. I took my chance and jumped quickly get a closer look at them, and then I saw it!

They were playing with each other's mouths! As soon as they saw me, they turned pale with fear and ran in different directions. I wondered what kind of hideous game I had just seen. This whole time, I was thinking they were doing something mysterious, so it was disappointing to find out that they had just been playing some stupid lip game.

Once the two of them had regained some confidence, they came close to each other again. The girl then started fighting with the boy.

"You kept saying that you would protect me from anything and never leave me alone. All it takes is one dog jumping at us for you to abandon me and run away! Is this your love? You liar! You cheater!", she emphasised.

The boy kept trying to make excuses, but the girl stayed angry at him. I didn't know what happened, but we saw them lock arms and go back happily after some time. Garima then criticised Mom for what had just happened.

"I'm sure you did that deliberately. Whenever you see these lovebirds, you always talk about how many of them have gathered here. I know you and your naughty ideas, but what would have happened if Sultan would have bitten them?"

Mom confidently said that she was sure of my non-violent nature.

"I just wanted to have some fun," she said with a cute smile.

I then understood everything. I used to think that Mom was a serious person, so it was surprising to learn that she had such a naughty side. And I now understood that the couples weren't brothers and sisters, they were lovers! They were playing weird games with their mouths on each other. After this episode I came to know that Lodhi Garden was a lovers' point too.

It was indeed a very entertaining episode.

This is how our walk continued with lot of fun and entertainment. The walks at Lodhi Garden had made me physically fit and active. Now, I could see the outside world on a daily basis, which broke the monotony of my routine. I used to feel fresh and rejuvenated after our walks. Even when I got very hot, Mom would give me cold water in my bowl and I would feel much better. Lodhi Garden had added a lot to my knowledge: it was here that I learnt about ducks and young couples, saw many different animals and birds and saw people doing all kinds of activities.

It was like seeing an entirely new world!

Chapter 56

Puppichino, the Restaurant

One Sunday morning, all of us were sitting in the living room. Mom was sitting at the dining table and reading the newspaper. Suddenly, she called out to Garima with excitement. When Garima came, she told her to read about a restaurant.

"See that? It says a new restaurant has opened recently, in Delhi, in Shahpur Jat and it's made for dogs. They have separate menus for dogs and people. I'm thinking we should go here with Sultan. It'll be a different experience, no? Call them and book a table for us today."

Garima was excited to see it, too, and called the number she saw in the newspaper. She looked quite disappointed when her conversation was over as she turned to Mom to tell her that the restaurant was fully booked today. Mom was still enthusiastic to go to the restaurant, and she asked Garima to book a table for next Sunday, which she did successfully.

I felt really happy, too. It was very exciting to know that I was going to be dining out with my family for the first time and that I would be served food made especially for me.

Finally, next Sunday came and we left to go to the restaurant, "Puppichino". It was very far from where we lived and it took us quite a long time to reach there. After a long wait, we finally arrived. As everyone was getting out of the car, Papa took my leash in one hand and a stick in the other. Suddenly, a lot of dogs appeared out of nowhere and started barking loudly at me. I got scared, but Papa was well prepared for our unwanted welcome and shooed them away with the stick. We started walking towards the restaurant and Papa asked a man for directions on our way there. Once we arrived, we entered a lift and went up.

The lift opened up and we took a right to walk into the restaurant. I was welcomed by two nice girls and their father. It really felt like a V.I.P.'s welcome! The restaurant looked simple but colorful and nice. The walls were covered with pictures of pets with their people. There was a small door near the counter that led to a play area for dogs with two trainers inside. I peeped over the door and saw a big dog the trainers called "Simba". As I was looking at her, Mom told me that she was a husky. The owner allowed me to go inside, and I went in to see Simba. She seemed busy playing with the trainers, though, so I quickly left and joined my family again. Everyone was looking at the menu and getting ready to order food. The idea of eating delicious food was much more exciting than playing with Simba, so I stayed with my family as they placed orders. One of the owner's daughters came over to our table and started taking everyone's order. Mom asked her for some advice before ordering my meal, and the girl helped her out, she also ordered one pizza packed up for Gabbar.

We waited for a little bit, and to my surprise, I was the first one to be served. I was given a bowl of chicken soup that I finished in no time. It was delicious, but there was more! One by one, delicacies were brought for me and given to me to eat. The best part was that I was served by the owner himself because my family was eating their food and he didn't want them to be disturbed. I was overwhelmed to see all the love he had for animals.

As I was eating, a few young girls and boys came up to us. The girls started complimenting me and sweet-talking me. One of them went to Madhav and asked what my name was.

"Thanks for the compliments. His name is Sultan."

"Hi, Sultan!", the girl said as she turned around to face me.

"Look how handsome you are! Your hair is so shiny and soft!"

Then they all took out their phones and started taking pictures of me. I felt very special, but also very nervous because I had never been surrounded by so many young girls in this way. It made me blush a little, thank God, they couldn't see my red cheeks because of my black colour. I was on cloud nine for being treated like a star!

We stayed there for a couple more hours and walked out after paying the bill. The whole time, I had to go pee really bad and I had to hold it in because I knew I couldn't pee inside the restaurant. As we were standing in front of the elevator, however, I just couldn't hold it in any longer and started peeing then there. I felt very bad as I did, but I had no control anymore. When I was finished, Papa went back inside the restaurant. I heard him talking to one of the girls.

"I'm so sorry, but my dog peed right outside. Could I get some water to clean it?"

The owner politely said not to worry and called out someone's name. Papa said that he didn't need to get anyone else to clean it and that since I was his dog, cleaning up after me was his responsibility. The owner said that their restaurant was made to cater to pets' needs and that cleaning up after the pets was their duty. I then saw a woman come out with a mop and a bucket, and she cleaned up my pee without any signs of disgust on her face. Papa walked out soon after and thanked her. I, too, thanked both of them in my heart. The lift doors opened and all of us went inside.

On our way back to the car, I thought about what a good time I had in the restaurant. It was really nice to go to a restaurant made specifically for pets like myself and I wished that many more restaurants like that one would open up soon so we wouldn't have to go somewhere so far away just for me to be able to come.

We went to Puppichino three or four more times. Once, we went there to celebrate my birthday. When Mom told the owners that it was my birthday, they made a special pizza for me, and the soup was complimentary. Garima and Madhav bought a bandana for me. I wore one for the first time and thought I looked very handsome in it. I deserved to feel special because it was my birthday. We had another pizza packed up to give to Gabbar, and then we left to go home.

I must say that whenever we went to 'puppichino', it used to be a memorable day indeed.

When Garima went to his house to give Gabbar his treat, Jasmine Aunty gave her my birthday gift. I was glad to get it and felt very thankful to Jasmine Aunty and Gabbar. She always gave me nice gifts on my birthday. It was clear that she spent time picking out things that would be useful for me. I always felt excited to find out what she had gotten me.

My family was discussing the experience at Puppichino. Mom was very satisfied to finally know a place where she could take me to eat with her. Madhav talked to her about other countries.

"You know, in developed countries, the culture around pets is entirely different. They don't have so many restrictions on them and they can be taken to most public places. They probably have a lot more 'Puppichinos' there… everyone there understands that pets are a part of their family."

Mom nodded her head in agreement.

"We need more restaurants like this. The government should let people bring their pets onto trains and buses if they're well trained. We don't know if our country will become pet friendly like the west, but if the government ever allows pets to travel, we can take Sultan on the train with us and go places."

I agreed with both of them. All I wanted when my family went on vacation anywhere was to go with them, but if they took planes or trains then I could never go with them.

Chapter 57

Gabbar Got Terminally Ill

Several months had passed by with life going on as normal. One day, Jasmine Aunty called Mom. She asked her to come over and bring me with her. Garima and Mom took me with them to Jasmine Aunty's door. Garima rang the bell and their helper opened the door. He asked us all to go to Jasmine Aunty's bedroom, which surprised all of us. Until now, we had always sat in the living room. Hesitatingly, we walked over to the bedroom and we were surprised to see three or four people already there. Mom called out to Jasmine Aunty, and she asked us to sit with her. She called out to me in particular.

"Sultan, come sit with Gabbar. He wants to see you."

Gabbar was lying on the floor with a drip in his leg. There was a piece of cloth next to his head. Jasmine Aunty lifted it to show it to us, and everyone was shocked to see it soaked in blood. Mom's voice shook as she asked Jasmine Aunty what was happening.

"Acute kidney failure."

She said that this could be the last time Gabbar would see any of us and that she wanted Gabbar to see me especially because I was Gabbar's only friend in the colony.

"Gabbar? Open your eyes, baby. Look, Sultan has come to meet you."

Gabbar blinked his eyes at me. It felt like he was acknowledging my presence. Jasmine Aunty told us that the blood was from Gabbar throwing up. She lifted his arm to show parts of his skin filled with water. After sitting there for an hour, we went back home with heavy hearts. In the evening, once Papa was home, Mom told him everything. Papa expressed his grief and sorrow for Gabbar in a very low and sad tone.

The next morning, we got another call. Jasmine Aunty said that it was time to say goodbye to Gabbar. All of us rushed over to their house. I felt a kind of nervousness I had never felt before. It felt like my stomach was hollow and heavy at the same time. It was very difficult to say goodbye to a beloved friend.

We went into Gabbar's room, where he was lying on the floor, motionless. I was pained to see him in a poor condition. He had a *Tilak* on his forehead and a flower garland around his neck. Aunty said that the garland was brought from a temple named "Pushkar Temple" in Ajmer, and that it was their blessing to him. She called out to him once again.

"Look, baby. Sultan is here to say bye to you."

He blinked at me again, like before. I was happy to know that he could still hear and see me, but knowing that this was my last goodbye made it a painful experience.

I had never felt what it was like to see someone close to you die. I knew for sure that death was a permanent separation and that I would never be able to see Gabbar again. This thought filled me with a feeling of deep sorrow. The fear of death gripped my heart. I had suffered unbearable separation before, and that was only for one day.

If that had left an unforgettable imprint on my mind, how would Gabbar's family bear permanent separation?

"Will they be able to cope with this loss?", I thought.

It was a Sunday morning, so both Gabbar's dad and my Papa were also there. Aunty told Gabbar that he had given so much to their family that they could never pay him back. She showed us a photo album with lots of pictures of him in it. As she flipped through the pages, she tried to hide her tears to no avail. After some time, all of us said Goodbye to Gabbar but as Papa and Garima accompanied him until the last moment, Mom, Madhav, and I returned to our house and gathered on the balcony to catch one final glimpse of him. Gradually, we watched as the others emerged from the building, signaling their departure.

"BYE, GABBAR! WE LOVE YOU!" Mom's voice boomed louder than ever before, echoing through the air. Only Jasmine Aunty turned back, offering a wave of farewell. Gabbar and his family settled into their car, while Papa and Garima occupied ours. We continued to stare, longing for a lingering connection until they disappeared from sight.

Hours later, Papa and Garima returned home, visibly affected by the events that transpired. They took showers to cleanse themselves, and it was then that Garima shared with Mom the details of Gabbar's final moments. She explained that Gabbar had been taken to a clinic, where a compassionate doctor administered an injection to alleviate his pain. Subsequently, they transported him to his burial place in Dwarka.

Garima revealed that tears welled up in Papa's eyes as they bid their final farewell during the burial. It was at that moment that memories of my dear friend, my lifelong companion, flooded my mind. I couldn't help but reminisce about the time I first visited Gabbar's house and savored his soup. The recollections enveloped me, evoking a bittersweet blend of nostalgia and sorrow.

"Why do we forge connections and make friends, only to face inevitable separation?" I pondered, grappling with the unanswered question that lingered within me. Despite my contemplation, no satisfying response emerged.

Chapter 58

My Family's Trips

One day I heard mom, dad and Garima discussing about a family trip they were wanting to take for three days. I immediately understood and that I would have to spend some days with Meena and Mahinder alone. Mom called out to me to tell me about it.

"Sultan, our trip is to the holy city of Benaras. We're going only for three days, and we'll be back on the fourth day, so we won't be gone long. I know that you'll miss us, but we can't take you with us on the train unless we put you in the luggage room and I just can't do that. It has no A.C. I don't want you to suffer like that. Besides, we wouldn't be able to take you with us to the temples, either. You can stay in the comfort of our house with the A.C."

The next day, I heard Papa talking to Madhav about the trip.

"Madhav, why don't you accompany us? Why do you want to stay alone in the house? Stop being stubborn and come with your family."

"Papa, I really have absolutely no interest in visiting temples and religious places. I'll just stay here and deepen my bond with Sultan. You guys go have fun."

Papa knew that there was no point in arguing with Madhav once he made up his mind about something. When

I heard Madhav say that he wanted to stay behind with me, I found him to be very considerate.

All three of them were gathered in the living room and preparing to leave. They gave me lots of kisses and set their goodbyes. Mom told me to enjoy my stay with Madhav, and that he wanted to spend some quality time with me.

Madhav and I had a great time together. We would go to Lodhi Garden evening and our time there would somehow be fun and relaxing at the same time. Madhav always kept me engaged in one game or another, and we had a lot of fun playing together. On the second afternoon after Mom, Garima, and Papa had left, we heard the doorbell ring. Madhav opened the door and we were surprised to see everyone had already returned.

"Wasn't your trip supposed to take three days? Why did you come back so soon?"

Garima said that they all missed Sultan too much, and decided to cancel the third day of their trip to return home. Madhav teased her and said that they only missed me, not him.

"You chose to stay here. Sultan was compelled to stay here. If our government wasn't so heartless, we could have brought him with us. Now, will you allow us to enter the house or not?", Mom asked.

"Yes, please come in," Madhav said as he stepped aside. "Treat this house as your own."

Everyone started laughing. They walked in and started petting me, caressing me, and playing with me. I couldn't stop wagging my tail, I was so happy to see everyone again! They all went inside to unpack all their bags, and so our daily routine started once again.

Several months later, Mom brought up another trip to me. "Sultan, we're planning a family trip to Goa but unfortunately we won't be able to take you with us. We're going there by plane and if you accompany us, they will sedate you. You'll be put in a cage and kept with the cargo. I can't put your life in danger like that, so you need to stay home. We'll be gone for six days. Don't worry, Meena and Mahinder will take care of you." she said.

I licked her hands to show her my approval, and she seemed satisfied with my gesture.

Two days later, everyone was packing up their luggage again. Garima and Madhav tried to reassure me with kind words, telling me that I shouldn't feel sad or alone in their absence. Mom gave instructions to Meena and Mahinder about how to care for me. She was telling them to be careful and not let me out of their sight for even a minute. They assured her that they would take the best care of me in her absence.

The next day, my family said goodbye to me and the helpers. Papa told me that they would see me again in six days and then they left for Goa. In their absence, Meena and Mahinder took really good care of me. They used to play with me and Meena groomed me when he had spare time. We also started spending more time in Lodhi Garden.

After a few days, the doorbell rang again and Meena opened the door to see everyone standing outside, much to his surprise. Everyone walked inside and Madhav ran to me and started kissing me. I couldn't stop wagging my tail out of joy! Meena went to the kitchen and brought water for everyone. As he was giving water to Mom, he asked her about her return.

"Madam, you said that it was a six-day trip, but you're back after only four days. How come?"

Papa smiled and told him that everything had gone fine, they were just missing me badly. When they saw the kids writing "Sultan" on the beach with sad expressions on their faces, they decided to cut the trip short and come back early.

Everyone started showing me love and my tail kept wagging side to side. Garima said that whenever they would see a dog, it would remind them of me. She said that one dog started sniffing her as if it had picked up my scent and they became friends. I was glad to hear that I had a family that loved me so much they couldn't bear to be away from me for long.

Life was going on comfortably as everyone resumed their daily routine.

Chapter 59

More Sad News

A few days later, mom received a distressing phone call on railway phone. Railway phone rang and she picked it up. I sat beside her and listened to her side of the situation, and I figured out that it was Mrs. Lalchand on the other side.

"What are you saying? Flunky is gone!?"

Mom sounded shocked. "How could that happen? She was just eight years old..."

After keeping the phone down, she told Garima and I that Flunky had passed away from kidney failure. Gabbar had passed away from kidney failure, too, but he was fourteen years old when Flunky was only eight. Mom told us that it had happened when they were all in Goa. Even though I had only met her a few times, I still felt very sorry for her and her family. She was only eight years old and it was too soon for her to go. This was another loss for me in the colony!

The next day, Mom, Garima, and I went to Mrs. Lalchand's house to express our condolences and grieve with her. We went in and sat down with her. For a few seconds, there was a sad silence. Mom spoke up first.

"We're so sad to hear this shocking news. She was so young... I still remember the days in Ferozpur when she was just a little puppy. She would lick our feet under the dining table. I still can't believe this has happened. God give her soul peace..."

Mrs. Lalchand pointed her finger at a wall. When we looked at it, we saw a picture of Flunky on it, with a garland around the frame. She broke down crying and became inconsolable. Mom tried to make her feel better but it didn't work. After some time, she drank some water and tried to regain her composure. She got up and went into her kitchen, coming out with a tray of snacks for us.

Neither Mom nor Garima touched any of the food. Mrs. Lalchand asked me to have snacks, but I didn't eat anything either. She took a biscuit in her hand and brought it to my face to get me to eat it, but I turned my face away.

"He's so intelligent. These are his favourite biscuits, and he used to eat them happily, but today he isn't even smelling this. Did you tell him not to eat anything because this isn't a routine visit?", she asked Mom.

"No, no! Not at all! I didn't even know that you would bring snacks for us on this occasion. I didn't give him any instructions, believe me."

Mrs. Lalchand gave her a half-hearted smile.

"I'm sorry. I casually blurted that out but I didn't mean anything by it. If anything, I'm glad that Sultan understands the gravity of the matter."

She narrated the story of Flunky's sickness and how she passed. When she was finished, she turned to look at me.

"Sultan, from now on you are my child. Whenever I miss Flunky, I will come to your house and spend some time with you."

We sat there for some more time and then left to go back home.

I never knew that my family had known Flunky since before I came into their lives. They used to live next to each other and the kids had known Flunky since they were children. I now better understood their feelings of loss.

After that day, Mrs. Lalchand started visiting our house. In the beginning, she would visit at least once a week, but as time went on the gap between her visits started to get bigger. Mom observed this and brought it up to Garima.

"Earlier, Mrs. Lalchand used to visit us weekly. It's now been one month since she's come over. I think it's a positive sign. She's starting to cope with Flunky's loss. I'm happy for her. You know, her daughter offered to bring another puppy for her, but she refused. She told her that she wants to devote her time to taking care of street dogs, and she has started feeding them and their puppies."

Garima agreed with Mom and said that Mrs. Lalchand was setting an example for dog lovers. Mom excitedly said to Garima, "I have never shared with you earlier, seeing Mrs. Lalchand reminds me of my Principal, Madam Anjali Aggarwal. I have never heard of such a dog lover. At one point of time she had twenty three pet dogs. She has also kept several kennels outside her mansion, meant for street dogs. Though she has several domestic helpers but she herself feeds street dogs. Have you ever heard of such a dog lover?" Garima said, "This is great. Amazing!"

When I heard that Mrs. Lalchand was taking care of street dogs, I became an admirer. After listening to Mom, I also became a great fan of my Mom's Principal. I was impressed with her dedication to helping the dogs that no one else would help.

Chapter 60

Garima Joined A New University

One day, I heard, Garima was arguing with Mom. She said to Mom, "Right from the beginning, I have been telling you that I don't want to study here. Why don't both of you try to understand my feelings, I don't want to study here. Right from my school days, I wanted to go abroad to study but you have always discouraged me. What will happen if one day, I tell you that now onwards I won't go to my present college." When Mom heard this, she said, "If you have any problem, then speak to your Papa, if he does not have any problem I don't mind. Please speak to him."

I guessed that Garima must have spoken to Papa because next day he asked Mom to find out about good foreign universities. From that day only, Mom started reading newspaper after coming back from school. She used to give me some time first, then she used to get busy with the newspaper. This routine continued for some days, one day she asked Meena to bring scissors. She cut something from the newspaper, then she took her phone and spoke to somebody. I couldn't understand anything but I had heard Garima's name several times in the conversation. She was looking very happy when her conversation was over, I guessed that there might be some good news for Garima.

After a few minutes, she herself spoke to me, "Sultan, I know you won't like this news because you love Garima too much. It might be difficult for you to live without her but we might have to bear this separation for her better future. Today, I spoke to an agency, they have said that there are good chances that she might get admission in a very reputed foreign university. I am so happy." I was listening to many words for the first time so I couldn't understand the meaning fully but I understood that Garima's wish might be fulfilled. Though I felt sad that Garima will go to a far-off place but I was satisfied that she would be happy.

Mom and Papa visited several places, checked about the agency and the university. They also got busy in doing a lot of paper work. One day, Garima got a phone call that her admission was confirmed, she hugged me out of joy. Then she rang up Mom and informed about the good news. When her conversation was over she said to me, "I am sorry that I will have to leave you here only. Actually, I am going on student visa so I can't take you with. Believe me, Sultan, I want to make my future in a particular field, so I will have to go there. Don't worry I will keep visiting whenever I get a vacation." Her last sentence gave me some relief otherwise I had thought that she was leaving forever.

After some days, Garima got admission in a foreign University in a far-off country. Mom and Garima got busy in shopping and started preparing for her journey and her stay. They also bought a big suitcase and one big bag. They started keeping the things on one bed, before going to the market Mom used to give a lot of instructions to both Meena and Mahinder. I had come to realise that actually Garima was going to a far-off country, I couldn't imagine my life without her. I started recalling the good time that I had spent with Garima. I especially remembered how she brought me to this family and how she was removing my ticks on my first day in the family. I felt like crying but soon I consoled myself that maybe it was necessary for her good future. This made me feel better.

My family threw a farewell dinner to our close relatives. Anju aunty, her family members and Devesh uncle came with his entire family. This time, a very little cute puppy also came with him. He was indeed very sweet, having a thick fur coat on his body and his eyes were round like very small balls. His hair was falling on his face so they were tied with a flat hair pin on his head, Devesh uncle introduced the puppy to all of us. He said, "Meet our cute puppy, Shifu. He is the youngest member of our family." Everyone congratulated him and Garima said to him, "He is cute, he looks like a ball of wool. Which breed is this?" Uncle briefly replied, "He is shitzu, a Chinese breed." Everyone started showering love on this cute puppy.

I also wanted to show my love to him, after everyone was through, he himself came running to me. We sniffed each other's nose then we started licking each other's genitals and kept on with this activity for a long period. Kabir, uncle's son said, "Why they are licking each other." His mother said, "They are saying hello to each other. It's their hello." He immediately said in surprise, "Will they will keep saying hello to each other for two hours. Very long hello!!!" Everyone started laughing but we kept on with our activity unaffected by the comment. After some time kebabas were served and we got our dog appropriate non-vegetarian food. It was a nice evening, all of us enjoyed thoroughly. Then everybody said bye to each other and all the guests left. The next day, finally the day had arrived for Garima to leave. She said to me in a very affectionate tone, "I would miss you a lot. I don't know how I will learn to live without you." The she gave me a loving caress on my back, I thought, "I also can't imagine my life without you. I am thankful to you for giving me such an amazing family." Papa intervened and said that we were getting late and we should start early. Meena and Madhav picked up the luggage and we started for the airport. When we had reached the airport, she said a final bye to us and went inside.

When we came back from the airport, I felt that the entire house was filled with some kind of emptiness. Suddenly my attention got diverted, when I heard Mom. She said to Papa, "When will she speak to us? How will we ensure that she reaches her destination safely?" Papa said to her, "Don't worry. She will speak to us once she reaches Singapore. I have got my international call services activated and I have told her about this." I immediately put a check on my thought process, I thought instead of missing her, I should have thought about her safety first.

All of us were eagerly waiting for her phone call, we were sitting in the study room. Mom was feeling very restless, we did not receive any phone call from Garima. Suddenly we heard a beep on Papa's phone, Papa immediately picked up his phone. He said, "There's no phone call but one message has come that she has boarded the connecting flight from Singapore. She will speak to us once she reaches her destination. So there is nothing to worry about, you can do your work without any tension."

Everyone got busy in their own work, I also sat in one corner. When Madhav saw this, he came to me and started talking to me. He said, "Are you missing Garima? All of us are missing her, you know she used to tease me a lot. Mom used to get very upset but I never felt bad. Whenever she used to tease me, this used to add spice to my life. Don't worry, I am with you, I will spend all my free time with you." His words gave me some solace, I felt happy that now onwards he will spend some more time with me. The next day, we got a phone call from Garima and I was surprised that we could see her on the phone. She could also see us, she spoke to all the members of the family one by one. She was looking very happy and excited, I was also very excited to see her though she was sitting in a far-off country. Meena and Mahinder also expressed their desire to speak to her. Mom handed over the mobile phone to them, they also spoke to her and asked about her welfare. There was a festival like environment in the family, now onwards it became a routine to receive a phone call from Garima in the afternoon. This is how we were in constant touch despite being so far from each other.

After a few days, Papa came back from his office and called everyone in the living room. He was looking very stressed, all of us were anxious to listen to him. Finally, he broke the silence and said, "I have a good news and bad news. Good news is that I have got a promotion, now my rank would be of Inspector General but I will have to move to Guwahati, Assam." Everyone congratulated him, mom said, "Don't worry. I will take care of the household here in Delhi. You are going on a promotion so go and join there with a carefree mind." Papa thanked Mom immensely and said, "I was getting tensed about how you would react. Now I can join without any tension."

Papa started packing his luggage the very next day and a few days later, he left for Guwahati. Now it was only me, Madhav and Mom in the house and, though we used to miss him a lot but everyone tried to look normal and soon resumed our normal routine.

Chapter 61

Madhav Also Went Abroad

Garima visited us again after a very long time. When she arrived, there was a festival-like environment in the house. Every day was so full of fun and joy! The three of us played a lot together. Papa visited too and started taking me for morning walks again and our apple parties resumed!

Garima had come to stay for one month and we didn't realize how fast all the days would pass. Before I knew it, the day had come when she had started packing her luggage. I immediately understood that it meant that she would soon leave for her college. My apprehensions proved to be right because after a few days, there came a night when she hugged me tightly and told me she was going to leave.

"My dear Sultan! The time has come for me to say bye to you. I have to leave tomorrow morning..."

She hugged me tightly and started caressing me on my back. We said good night to each other. Madhav then came into the room out of nowhere.

"Garima! Let's play hide and seek with Sultan before you go to bed. I have my board exams and I'll also leave for college, so we don't know when we'll get the chance to play together again. Let's make this day a memorable one!"

Garima readily agreed and we played together for quite a long time, eventually getting tired and falling asleep. I, however, had a very restless night. I kept thinking about how Madhav said that he also had plans to go abroad and I grew worried, not knowing who would keep me company after Madhav's absence.

After some hours passed, Papa came in to wake us up to leave for the airport. Everyone got ready and we dropped Garima off at the airport and came back. The moment we entered, the house felt empty already. Papa left to go back to Assam the next morning, too.

Everyone tried to look normal but Papa's absence only added to an awkward stillness in the entire house.

The next day, after Mom left for her school, Bajrang Sir arrived to tutor Madhav. He would tutor Madhav in two subjects and worked very hard to teach him. Madhav studied seriously so he now had less time to play with me, but I didn't mind. Finally, the day of his exams came and after giving his exams, he started to spend much more time with me. After a few days, it became routine for Mom to take Madhav shopping every now and then. They would tell me that they were leaving to go shopping and come back a few hours later with food for me. I really appreciated this gesture of kindness because I knew that the shops they went to wouldn't allow me to enter in with them.

When Madhav's result was declared, I saw preparations for his departure gradually pick up speed. It led me to start mentally preparing myself for another separation. Every evening, Madhav would sit behind me and gently pet me. He never uttered a word but his touch and manner conveyed the feeling that he loved me a lot. Perhaps I was also able to convey the same...

The days passed, and one day Papa showed up at the door, much to my surprise. I ran towards him and my tail started to wag wildly. Papa gave me a big hug and then Madhav came out and gave Papa a hug. Papa affectionately reminded him about his plans.

"So my boy is ready to fly. Young man, your flight will only stop at one place for refueling. When you reach your destination, get a local number as fast as you can and keep us posted. I am here for four days just to help you with your remaining shopping. After sending you off, I will leave to go back to work."

Hearing this, Madhav seemed concerned.

"What about Mummy and Sultan? Will they stay here by themselves?"

He paused for an answer, but Papa didn't say anything so he spoke again.

"Is that fair?"

"My son, Assam is heavily flooded. No trains are running and I don't want to take Sultan on a plane because they will sedate him and put him with the cargo which will be too uncomfortable and dangerous for him. We will have to wait for train routes to start up again. I hope you understand and appreciate my logic here."

Madhav slowly nodded his head and told Papa that he was right.

Papa and Madhav got busy shopping the next day. I now clearly understood that Madhav would only be here with us for a few more days. Later, at night, he came to me and told me that he would be leaving in four days. He said that he wanted to take me along with him but because he was only going as a student, nobody would let him bring me along. It hurt to know that he was going to be leaving me behind but it was somewhat reassuring to hear the reason…

The night before his departure, Madhav came to me in the living room and hugged me tightly. I felt tears falling from his eyes but he didn't utter a single word the whole time he held me. I didn't hear him talk but I still felt the immense love he had for me.

Finally, a few minutes passed and he started to speak.

"Sultan, I loved you the moment you came into our house. I asked Garima to let us keep you many, many times but everything failed. Some strange and unlikely things happened and finally changed Mummy's heart. Now you're a part of our family, and we can't imagine life without you."

I reflected on how things happened and how glad I was to be with my family.

"I will miss your fleshy thighs… sorry. I don't mean to scare you, I just don't know how to express my feelings. You know, mom likes your ears a lot. She keeps saying she wants to chew on them. I don't know, I guess we're just trying to express your cuteness in words!"

I was not scared, but I definitely found these compliments unique.

We left the next morning to go to the airport. Once we got there, Madhav gave me a kiss on my forehead and got out of the car. Papa and Madhav walked into the airport together while Mom and I waited in the car. After some time passed,

Papa came out of the airport alone and got back in the car. I had tried to mentally prepare myself for this separation, but it didn't work. We rode back home in silence. The next day, Papa left early in the morning to take a flight so he could go back to work. Now the only ones left at home were Mom and I, with Meena and Mahinder for company.

Mom stopped going to school a few months later. She used to stay at home all day. It was a difficult time for both of us because both of us were struggling with loneliness. Mom started spending more time with me and taking extra care for me. I wanted to talk back to her but she couldn't understand my language. Many days passed by with no events and nothing exciting happening. Life without three members of our family seemed very dull and boring. "Are we going to spend the rest of our lives like this?", I would think to myself.

I began to wonder why Papa was not visiting us anymore. One morning, when Mom and I were sitting in the living room, the phone began to ring. Mom picked up the phone and had a conversation with the person on the other side for a long time. When the call was over, she happily looked at me and told me that we were moving!

"Sultan! Soon we will be joining your Papa in Assam. Finally, the wait is over!"

She then called Mahinder and Meena and briefed them about our journey. She was so excited that she hugged me several times, again and again! I, too, was overjoyed to see her be happy again. Finally, something was going to happen!

Chapter 62

Journey to a Far-Off Place

A couple of days after the phone call with Papa, Mom started to get ready for our eventual departure. She told Meena to buy a new leash and some packed food for me.

"I'm going to the local market with Mahinder to buy a new bag for Sultan. Meena, you go to Shankar Market and buy what I told you. We have a lot of work to do, and not that much time."

Soon, all three of them got ready and left to do their shopping.

A few hours later, everyone returned with new things. Mom and Mahinder had brought a red bag and Meena had bought me a shiny new leash and dry food. Mom looked surprised when she saw the price tag on the leash.

"Meena, why did you go with such an expensive leash?"

"Our sir has become a V.I.P. now, so Sultan needs to have a luxury belt Madam."

Mom and Mahinder smiled at his response. She then told everyone to start rounding up my things, telling them that we were all going to leave the day after tomorrow. Everybody made themselves busy as I silently watched and followed them around.

Finally, the day had arrived. Vijender and Meena picked up all the bags and we went down to get in the car. Soon we set off and after a few minutes of riding in the car, we arrived at a strange place that was very crowded and very loud. Meena took my leash and we got out. Some people came up to us, introducing themselves as "Dobi" and "Satish". They took our luggage and we started following them as they walked. As we walked, I saw what looked like a really, really long red car. I wondered what it was.

I looked back at Mom with amazement, and it seemed she read my mind because she told me what I was looking at.

"Sultan, this is a train. It's called the Rajdhani Express. We're going to get on a train like that and it will take us to your Papa really fast! We'll travel together, just you and me. It's going to be a fun day!"

I was still amazed by the size of the train. I had no idea how it could even exist!

It was a very hot day, so I soon began puffing and panting. Meena went to a nearby stand and bought a bottle of water, bringing it to me. After having a relieving drink, I looked up to see many people staring at me as if they had never seen a handsome dog before. Soon, the red train we were going to get in arrived at the platform in front of us. After Dobi yelled something, two people came running towards us. They were wearing a red uniform and looked like they were going to help us. When they caught up to us, they picked up our luggage! I thought they might try to run away with our things so I got ready to chase and catch them.

To my surprise, they just quietly stood there after picking up our things. Dobi then asked us to walk with him to the part of the train we were going to get on. We walked for a few minutes and then finally arrived at the part of the train we were going to board! After Mom and I got on, I looked around to see where we were. Everything was new to me and I saw many things I hadn't seen before. Meena was holding my leash as he got on with me and the two coolies carried our luggage. All of us walked until Meena slid a door open and we finally went inside our coupe! Mom asked the coolies to put my bag down away from the other bags and Meena spread a bed sheet on one of the two seats that were there. Since there were only two, I understood that only Mom and I were going to sit there... Meena started patting my back, telling me to take care of myself in his absence. I thought to tell him to take care of our house in my absence and that I will miss him too, but it seemed like he read my mind because he responded before I could even say anything.

"Don't worry, Sultan. I will take care of myself and the house as well."

Suddenly, a loud and shrill whistle sounded and my ears rose in alertness.

Meena hurriedly said Namaste with folded hands and immediately left to get out of the train. I didn't understand why until a sudden and sharp jerk shook my body. I was about to fall down from my seat when Mom reached out and held me tightly. This was a completely new experience for me... I had travelled in cars before, but they had never moved with such force. I looked outside the window to see people still standing on the train platform, and then realized the train was slowly moving. It gradually picked up speed until it was so fast that we had left the entire train station far behind! And so our journey to a far-off place started!

Chapter 63

Train Journey

I felt very proud to be a member of my family. I thought, "How many animals get the chance to travel by train like this?", I thought. "If I tell other dogs about this, I'm sure they'll be jealous of me. I can't wait to tell Buzo and Bolt when I get back to Delhi!"

Dobi came into our cabin to tell Mom that his seat is near our coupe and that she could call him whenever she needed any help. He also told her that he would take me outside to relieve myself when we got to the next station. He then left, Mom went to close the door and we sat next to the window. Looking out of the window, I saw more trees than I had even seen at Lodhi Garden!

After some time passed, we heard a knock at the door. Mom went to open it and I saw a man outside who asked to see a ticket. Mom got the cricket out of her purse and showed it to him, and he left. Before Mom could close the door though, another man came up to her. He was holding a tray and asked Mom if she wanted tea or coffee as he walked into our coupe. Mom replied that she wanted coffee and the man poured her a cup. He then put a sandwich on the table and left. Mom gave me the sandwich to eat, which I devoured instantly and found quite unique in taste.

A while later, another waiter came and served us soup with bread and butter. I knew upon seeing the soup that I was going to get my share so my mouth started watering right away. Mom put half of the soup in my bowl and put it under a fan to let it cool. While we waited for the soup to cool down, she broke the soup sticks down into small pieces and gave them to me to eat. By the time I was done eating the soup sticks, the soup had cooled down enough so Mom gave it to me to have. Needless to say, I finished it in no time. It was so delicious and creamy!

I thought about how nice and generous the people in the Rajdhani were, since they treated a dog guest like myself so well and made me feel special. Mom poured her soup into a bowl and began to sip it. I stared out the window and saw huge fields with many people working on them. As I wondered what I was looking at, Mom explained it to me.

"Sultan, these are paddy fields. That's where we get rice from."

I used to think the big open spaces in Lodhi Garden were the biggest there were. How wrong I was! The paddy fields I was looking at seemed to go on forever.

As I admired the size of the paddy fields, I realized I needed to relieve myself. But where? Suddenly there was a knock at the door.

"Did the waiter bring more things to eat? I'm full, but I can make room for more!", I thought to myself. Mom went and opened the door, and to my disappointment it was just Dobi on the other side. He entered our coupe and put my leash on, telling Mom that a stop was coming and he would take me down. Mom approved and, when the train came to a stop a few minutes later, he took me outside the train to a secluded spot where I could relieve myself.

People stared at me as I walked back. I was starting to think no one outside of my family had ever seen a dog like me! Some people were getting scared of me for no reason and hurriedly moving out of our way. I didn't understand what they were so afraid of but I paid them no mind as we walked back and boarded the train again.

Dobi took me back to our coupe and took my leash off when we got back to Mom. As she did whenever I would come back from a walk, she gave me water to drink. I quickly drank the water and sat back down on the floor. Mom told me that Papa would soon be joining us, which I was very excited to hear! The very thought of meeting him again after such a long time was instantly exciting. The train started to move again and quickly reached full speed. Every now and then it would whistle a shrill and loud sound, which I had now gotten used to. I had also learnt to maintain my balance with the movement of the train.

After some time passed, a waiter came to us again, this time to take our order for dinner. Mom asked for two non-vegetarian meals. He then asked her what he should bring me and she said that some boiled chicken and two rotis would be enough. He noted our order down and left. Some minutes later, he came back with two plates and one bowl. Mom tore up the roti into pieces and put it in the bowl with the chicken. She then gave it to me to eat. As I ate dinner, I wondered why she had asked for two plates.

I soon understood that it must be for Papa. Mom must have been waiting for him because she had not opened the plates yet. As we waited, Dobi knocked at our door and came in. He began to put my leash on me again and I realized that he was going to take me out again and we were going to come to a stop once more. We went out and after I was done, we boarded the train again.

When I entered our coupe I was greeted with an amazing surprise. Papa was sitting right there! I finally got to see him again after so many days! I couldn't contain my joy and started jumping around, wagging my tail. Papa gave me lots of kisses on my head.

"I finally came to see you, *beta*! How is my son?"

Eventually I managed to calm down enough and regain my breath. Mom started setting the plates down for the two of them to eat dinner but Papa asked her about me before they could start.

"Have you given Sultan something to eat yet?" Mom smiled as she reassured him.

"Do you really think you have to worry about him when I am with him?"

Papa smiled and told her that he knew that as long as she was there with me, he had nothing to worry about. They smiled at each other and started having their meals.

A few minutes after they were finished with their meal, the waiter brought cups of ice cream, which I was overjoyed to see. After all of us had ice cream, we sat down near the window. It had become dark outside but I could still see distant lights. Mom seemed to realize what I was looking at and became excited.

"Sultan, are you looking at the shiny lights in the sky? Those are stars! There's so much pollution in Delhi that we barely even get to see a clear sky, let alone stars."

Seeing so many stars was wonderful! I kept admiring them until it got even darker and I started to feel sleepy, as did Papa. Mom switched off the lights and we went to our seats to sleep. Papa slept on the upper seat and Mom and I took the lower berth. The train's gentle movement made me feel like I was on a gentle swing and soon after lying down, I fell asleep.

We woke up to a knock on the door. The waiter had brought us our breakfast! Mom gave me my meal to eat first and then she and Papa started having their breakfast. When we were done, I went to sit near the window again. Looking outside, I saw many people sitting on the ground with bottles next to them. I couldn't understand why people would just squat on a field with water next to them until I saw some of them washing themselves with it! It was strange to see people pooping in open spaces like I used to!

Though the Rajdhani staff were very hospitable, they would always bring one thing or the other after a short interval. It was starting to get overwhelming and my enthusiasm for this train journey was starting to gradually fade away. I started feeling uneasy just idly sitting in the coupe, unable to walk around to properly stretch my muscles. I overheard Papa telling Mom that the training was running three hours late, which did nothing to cheer me up.

Looking out the window, I was surprised to see lots and lots of running water. It looked like the train was running on some huge metal construction, which made a strange and loud noise. When papa heard it, he sounded glad as he told Mom about it.

"We've reached the bridge. Soon, we will finally arrive at Guwahati station!"

Mom looked happy to know that we would soon reach our destination. I, too, felt relieved to know that this tiring journey was finally going to come to an end.

Chapter 64

Our New House

Mom started packing our luggage back up and our waiter came to us again with a plate. Whatever he had brought smelled really sweet which made me really eager to try some. When he put the food down, Mom reached into her purse and took out a big note of money to put on the tray for the waiter. He saluted Mom and went back with a smile on his face.

When Papa saw it, he asked Mom something.

"Was that a five hundred rupee note? Why give him such a big tip?"

"These waiters served Sultan so generously that I didn't even need to open the packet of food I bought for him. See?"

She showed Papa an unopened bag of dog food. Even though the packet was sealed, it smelled amazing. I agree with Mom, the waiters had been good to me so I didn't mind them getting more money than usual.

"Well, if they've been so good to my Sultan then they definitely deserve something extra. Isn't that so boy?", Papa said as he pet me and ruffled the hair on my head.

As he was playing with me, Dobi came in after knocking at the door. He started picking up our luggage and putting it near the door. Soon, the train came to a stop and four people in the same uniform Papa used to wear came to our coupe.

They gave Papa a salute and picked up our luggage. We got off the train and were escorted to a really big car. Dobi bid farewell to us and got in another car.

By the time our car started, it had become very dark. I was surprised to see a vehicle ahead of us escorting us to wherever we were going. Some time later, we finally arrived at our new house… Mom got down and entered a covered verandah. I got down with Papa and he led me to the house by my leash, but I didn't want to get in. I barked and tried to pull away. This wasn't my house! My house was in Delhi, and this wasn't it. I didn't want to go in there. Papa had to lift me up and carry me inside!

I met two strangers in the house who welcomed us. They were being nice to me but I didn't feel comfortable around them. Both this house and these people were alien to me. The strangers asked Mom what they should make for dinner and she said she wanted to go to the kitchen and look at the vegetables they had to decide. Seeing how normal Mom was acting made me realize that I had to act like a grown up like her or I would just suffer here. As I came to realize that, I saw Mom walk towards the kitchen and give the two new guys instructions about dinner for all of us.

In the meantime, Papa changed his clothes and came back to show me around the house. It was very big, with two lawns full of flowers and lots of tall trees. There were two water tanks and plenty of tiny plants around them. It made me happy to see so much greenery around what would become my house! The house was also bigger than I first thought.

"A big officer like my Papa deserves a big house like this", I thought.

"Sultan, this garden is for our kitchen. It's dark now so you can't see the vegetables, but I'll show it to you tomorrow. Let's go inside, your dinner must be ready now."

We soon got back inside and I saw mom mixing rotis in my bowl. It was nice to see a familiar sight and knowing that my dinner would soon be ready made me very happy. Once my dinner was served, I got to eating right away. I must have been hungrier than I thought because I gulped it down faster than usual. It was so fast that Mom had to tell me to slow down.

"Sultan, don't eat your food so quickly. You could choke and I don't know where I will find a doctor in this new place."

Hearing her advice, I immediately slowed my pace. I didn't want to create problems for her or myself. Once my meal was finished, Papa took me for a walk outside. After I had fully relieved myself, Papa walked me back inside.

I felt very tired from our long train journey. Mom led me inside to the bedroom where there was a mattress for me. I laid on the mattress but just couldn't fall asleep. I felt too awkward sleeping on a new surface in a new place. Both of my parents joined me in the room after eating their dinner. They sat on the bed and I started whining. Mom immediately understood that I wanted to get up on the bed with them. She asked me to jump up and I quickly joined them. Papa switched the lights off and Mom hugged me tightly. I felt so safe and comfortable that I immediately fell asleep. I had a dream where I saw Mahinder and Meena and they took me for a walk after giving me food. Suddenly, the dream was over and I was awake. Papa was already up and moving and Mom was not in the bedroom.

Chapter 65

My New Colony and I

I wanted to get down from the bed but it was too high for me, so I started whining. Papa immediately entered the room and gently brought me down. When he saw that I was wide awake, he gave me my breakfast. Then he tied the leash on my waist and took me for a walk. It was a very neat and clean colony, I noticed one thing that it was not crowded like Panchkuian Road Colony and there were hardly any street dog. It was a very green place, so many large trees, so many creepers which had enveloped the big trees. There were big and independent bunglows which were well protected by hedges. Papa took me to a beautiful club, there was a fountain in the midst of the lawn. The lawn was full of beautiful flowers, I had not seen so many flowers earlier. It's walls had attractive paintings on them, this looked much much more beautiful than our previous club which had plain walls and no greenery.

I found our new colony was well maintained, there were no multi story flats like we had in Delhi. Papa showed me something and said, "Sultan, these are hillocks. These have thick forest and leopards come from there." Papa continued, "Sultan, you can move freely in the open space of our house only during daytime. When it gets dark, leopards come in search of their prey."

I had heard the word 'leopard' for the first time so I didn't take that animal seriously. I had assumed that prey means pray, I wondered, "Does that leopard pray to God and worship like Papa does every morning?" Suddenly immense respect arose in my heart for such a religious animal, now I wanted to meet the leopard.

After a long walk we came back home and Papa gave me cold water. When I reached the verandah, I saw that Mom was reading a newspaper while sipping her tea. She asked me if I liked the place or not. She said, "Sultan, you had refused to enter the house yesterday. Do you like the place now? This is your new house and we are going to stay here now. See such big lawns, so many beautiful flowers. You have vast open space to roam around freely."

I nodded my head in agreement, in the meantime a big vehicle entered our house. The driver parked the vehicle near the verandah, seeing a vehicle so close to me, I wanted to jump in it and go for a ride. Suddenly Mom got up and asked me to sit in the vehicle so I happily sat in the vehicle. She also sat down beside me and asked the driver to show us the colony. We started to explore exploring the colony, Papa's Personal Security Officer started telling us about the colony. After a few minutes the driver stopped the vehicle near an isolated road and told Mom that the road led to General Manager's bunglow. He also said, "Madam, leopards frequently come here on this road and take away small animals like dogs, goats and eat them up. Our security staff sees leopards here, almost every night."

When I heard this, it seemed as if I had woke up from a deep slumber. I was thinking that the leopard was a genteel and religious animal. It eats goats and dogs, means my life was also in danger. I tried to recall Papa's words carefully and tried to derive their meaning, now I started dreading leopard. When Mom heard about the leopard, she said, "Sultan, you shouldn't worry about it because we will never leave you alone in the night and during the daytime you will always be surrounded by your Papa's staff. They will always protect you." These words gave immense solace to my heart.

After ten minutes we reached back to our house. Mom went inside and asked me also to get in. I obediently followed her, she went towards the kitchen and washed her hands. I sat down near the dining table, in the meantime Papa had finished his prayers and went inside to change his dress. When he came out I saw he was wearing his uniform and he was looking very handsome in it. He came and sat down on the dining chair and asked Brahmo, "Bring papaya for me and Sultan." Brahmo immediately served us papaya. Needless to say that I finished it within no time, it was very sweet and tasty. Mom also arrived there and the breakfast was served. I was sitting near the table, when Papa had finished, he gave one bite of his breakfast as usual. Then he said bye to both of us and left for his office.

After some time Mom said to me, "Sultan, you have seen the entire house but I have not. Let's go outside to see the house together." Mom and I went out to see the house around. The moment we stepped out, we were greeted by a tall man, he wished good morning to Mom. He introduced himself to Mom as Rajbongshi and asked her if she had seen the kitchen garden. When Mom said no, he said that he would like to show her the kitchen garden.

We started with cauliflowers and tomato plants, the garden was full of them. Some were getting over-riped so

Mom asked that they should be removed and the good ones be distributed among the staff, I liked her gesture very much. Our kitchen garden had almost everything from broccoli, potatoes, peas, bitter gourd, cabbage, spinach, mint, fenugreek plants, even garlic. Rajbongshi told Mom that this kitchen garden is result of hard work of Mandal alone. He used to do everything, from buying good quality seeds, sowing them and watering them with a bucket. Mom met him and admired his dedication and hard work.

There were so many papaya trees, laden with papayas, I immediately understood that Brahmo must have plucked them from these trees. We also saw very tall trees, I had never seen such tall trees not even in Lodhi Garden.

Mom pointed her finger towards those trees and said, "Look, Sultan, these are coconut trees and the tiny creatures which are climbing up and down are called squirrels." Suddenly one tiny coconut fell down in front of us, Mom picked it up to see if there was some water in it. But Rajbongshi told that squirrels had made a hole in the tender coconuts and had drunk the water. I raised my head to see the squirrels on the top, Oh My God, they were playing havoc with our coconuts, I felt like climbing up the tree and chasing them away but it was too tall for me to climb. After showing us the kitchen-garden Rajbongshi said that he will have to leave to go to the office.

Mom said O.K. and we turned back, we saw that there were some big trees and many middle sized animals with long tails, were sitting on them. Younger animals werejumping from one tree to another, some were pulling each other's tails. They were indeed very naughty, I liked there movements and fun loving activities very much. Perhaps Mom was also enjoying their activities intently, she told me that those animals were monkies and added something new to my general knowledge. After seeing them for a while, Mom sat down in the verandah and got busy with the newspapers. I sat down by her and soon I was fast asleep. After a while, I heard creaking noise of the door which Mom had opened, perhaps she wanted to go in. So I also got up and followed her inside the house. We entered the main room where she again got busy with another newspaper so I also laid down myself on the floor to resume my sleep. I got up when someone knocked at the door to tell Mom that my lunch was ready. I immediately got up and rushed towards the kitchen where I was served my lunch.

When I had finished, Brahmo took me to the backyard and tied the leash on my waist. He took me towards the main door perhaps he wanted to take me for a walk. Brahmo was a stranger for me and I just didn't want to go with a stranger. I started barking and whining desperately.

Finally Mom had to come to see, what the matter was. Brahmo told her that I was not willing to go for a walk with him. So Mom decided to accompany me, I felt relieved to see that. Then I snatched my leash, held it in my mouth and went towards mom, to my surprise, mom took hold of my leash. When I saw this pleasant development, I happily started going for the walk.

When we had reached a square, Mom must have seen something there. She asked Brahmo to change our direction but I did not let him do so. I became adamant to go in that direction only, then Mom asked Brahmo to shoo the goats away, I also looked in that direction. There was one grown up goat with her four calves. They were dark brown and beautiful, I noticed that they were gazing at me in surprise. Mom asked Brahmo that why they were staring at me, he giggled and said, "Perhaps they have not seen a jet black dog in their lives." I got very angry at this comment, what kind of person he was, how dare he comment on my colour in a derogatory manner? I felt like biting on his hand but couldn't do this because I was not aggressive by nature.

Anyways, I remembered that there were some goats, whose matter had to be solved. I thought I should ask them personally, so I suddenly started running in the same direction, Bramo stumbled and lost control over my leash. When the goats saw me running in their direction, they got afraid and started running in different directions. By this time Brahmo had reached there and took my leash in his hands. OMG! Mother goat was the first one to start running, leaving her calves behind. When the calves saw their mother running, they also started running helter skelter.

I wondered, "What king of mother is she? She left her calves alone when she perceived a danger looming around them." I was very sure that my mom would never leave me alone in danger. After some time, I had regained my breath. Though I was panting but I enjoyed chasing them because I had taught them a lesson for gazing at me unnecessarily. We resumed our walk and came back home, I was given cold water after reaching there. I came to the main bed-room and went to sleep.

Around two'o clock Papa's vehicle entered the complex and I got up with the sound, Mom also got up and went towards the dining table for lunch. Papa was already sitting there, I also went there and sat by their side. When they had finished eating Papa gave me one bite to eat. Though it wouldn't fill my stomach but used to give me joy and I always used to wait for the last bite after each meal. After finishing our lunch we came to the room, I and Papa went to sleep. Mom was sitting on the chair and reading a book. Soon I was fast asleep and I didn't realise, that when Papa had left. I got up, when Brahmo knocked at the door and asked Mom to send me for a walk. I went out, he took me to the backyard and tied leash on my waist. He took me out in the verandah and I started barking desperately. Finally Mom had to come out and accompany us.

Hurray, I had succeeded! I loved this kind of small victories of mine, I knew how to change Mom's decisions.

The sun was about to set and sky had become covered with thousands of crows flying from one tree to another making very loud and screeching noise. I had never seen so many crows in Delhi, I was surprised to see their number. We started for a walk and took the same route which we had taken earlier.

Around 7 o' clock I was given my dinner and I was taken for a walk inside the campus only. Mom asked Brahmo to carry a large bamboo stick, the sentry was also accompanying us. They were discussing that it was dark now and they had to be very cautious about the leopard. I got very scared and hurriedly relieved myself and we entered the house. By that time Papa had also arrived from the office. I ran out to welcome him and started barking out of joy, he started patting me on my back.

My daily routine used to start with papaya and breakfast, then a walk with papa. An outing after lunch with Mom and Brahmo, another outing a little before sunset, then dinner around 7 in the evening and then a walk inside the complex. If at all, I was taken outside after sunset, then sentry and Brahmo used to accompany me, with large bamboo sticks in their hands.

Life was going on smoothly with this routine.

Chapter 66

My New Companions

One Sunday, Mom went to the market to buy vegetables and some kitchen items while I and Papa were at home. Mom came back in the afternoon, she had also brought something very amazing and I think she had brought it for my company. She kept a small cage down and I saw, there were two small birds, which were very beautiful and they were making very melodious sound. I started looking at them in amazement, I had seen only pigeons and crows in Delhi but had never seen such small, cute and colourful birds earlier, they were indeed very charming. I liked them very much and I went near the cage, then started barking at them out of love. I also started clawing at the cage because I wanted them to come out and play with me. When mom saw this, she got afraid and kept the cage at a height.

Papa said to Mom, "Why have you brought these sweet birds, do you really want to keep them in cage? I can not believe, you can keep somebody in prison." Mom said, "I have brought these for Sultan. He will be happy to see them. Moreover these are ornamental they can not fly high so they are safe here from other bigger birds." He said o.k. and kept quiet but it was obvious from his face that he didn't want to imprison somebody.

I wanted to play with the birds but Brahmo had made a temporary arrangement for them in the living room. He fixed a wire on the wall and hanged the cage on the wire. Next day the birds were kept in the open in the morning and were given special feed. There was a small swing in the cage and the birds used to sit on that and take swings. I liked their movement and agility with which they used to move. One day when the cage was put in the open, I saw that no one was guarding the cage. I clawed it hard and the cage opened into three parts, fell down like a castle of sand and the birds flew out shoooo, within a blink of eye. Everybody present there was shocked to see this.

The birds started flying in different directions, I saw that they could fly really high. Mom became very sad to see this and said to Papa, "The shopkeeper had told me that the birds were ornamental. He had also said that cage was very sturdy and won't break so easily. Sultan's one paw and it got opened into pieces." Papa smiled and said, "Dear, it was a cage for small birds not for a lion." When I heard this I couldn't control my laughter in my heart.

Life was going on very smooth and everything was fine except for one thing, which was really very irritating. Actually Brahmo was very nice and caring, he really used to take care of me. He was very polite and he did everything to make me comfortable there but there was kumar also who really used to irritate me, he was very nagging. Whenever he would see me sitting somewhere, he would start saying, "Sultan brother, get up from here and sit there." If I would sit in that corner, after five minutes, he would again say, "Sultan, change your place. Come and sit here."

He used to say this whenever would see me, maybe ten times in a day or more. Mom had also noticed this so she tried to check Kumar, she asked him, not to keep repeating the same thing and stop irritating me. He said O.K. and improved his behaviour just for two-three days only. After a brief interval he again started saying the same thing. When Mom saw that he was not improving his behaviour, Mom brought the matter to Papa's notice and he also got very agitated. Then he strictly ordered Kumar to stop irritating me. After Papa's scolding he completely changed his behaviour and stopped bothering me altogether.

It had brought a big relief to me, now I could spend my day the way I wanted to!

Chapter 67

Heavy Rain and its Problems

When we had reached Guwahati, Mom had told me that rainy season was over and puja time was arriving soon. One Sunday morning when we were sitting in the verandah, Papa looked at the sky and told Mom, "I can see the sky and tell you that it is going to rain very soon. The clouds are very dark and approaching here very soon." Mom asked him that how he could be so sure and he replied, "I have been staying here for long and have learnt to read the sky. Soon we should send Sultan for a walk." Then he asked Brahmo to take me for a walk, he gave me my food and took me for a walk and soon I had relieved myself. When we were coming back, it started pouring, before we could reach our home it started raining heavily. Both of us got drenched badly, somehow we rushed to the house. Mom and Papa were eagerly waiting for us, Papa was holding a towel to wipe my body. He took me inside and wiped me thoroughly. Brahmo also wiped himself and entered the kitchen. We were sitting in the covered courtyard, it was thundering and raining very heavily.

I was enjoying the rain as I had not seen such heavy rain in Delhi. Mom was also overjoyed but Papa had an altogether different opinion. He said that he was fed up with so much of rain. I thought how he could be fed up with this, the weather had become very pleasant. Though it was afternoon but presense of clouds over the sky were indicating as if it was evening time. I thought that the rain would stop after sometime but it didn't. It kept raining for the whole day, that day had passed and next day also it didn't stop. My parents were worried about me, as how I could be sent for a walk, the sky was still very dark and there was no sign of the rain to take a break.

Sometimes it was raining heavily and sometimes not so heavily. Mom gave an idea that she should go to the market and buy a very small rain coat for me. Papa agreed with the idea, he asked Mom to get ready and go to the market. Mom left for the market, after some time the heavy rain turned into drizzling so Papa sent me for a walk, I was very happy because I was feeling tremendous pressure in my stomach. I was lucky that it kept drizzling and I came back home fully relieved. I had just entered and it started raining heavily again. Now I was also fed up with continuous rain just like my Papa was.

Mom had brought one raincoat for me. Next time when I had to go out Brahmo made me wear the raincoat. It was an altogether experience as it had trousers for my fore legs, I was feeling very awkward in it. But I didn't have any option, the raincoat was a great help, moreover Brahmo was keeping me fully covered under a big umbrella. The only problem was that we had to rush up, we used to be in a hurry to be back home.

I was facing lot of problem in going out for a walk and relieving myself. I think Papa was right that so much rain causes lots of problems. I was surprised to see that it rained continuously for four days without any break?

Finally the rain had stopped after four days and I was again able to go for my regular walk to my satisfaction.

Chapter 68

Hidden Talent Surfaced

I came to know in Guwahati that Mom was fond of learning new languages so one day, she asked Rajbongnshi to buy an introductry book of Assamese language. When she had got the book, she showed it me and said, "Sultan, see my new book. I will try to learn Assamese alphabets. I have given a cursory look at the entire book and have found that is has information about places of tourist attraction. I will find out which place is most attractive and we will visit that. O. K." I felt very happy to know that soon we will see a new place.

She came to know that there was a Madan Kamdev Temple near Guwahati. She told this to Papa and they planned to visit that temple on the coming Sunday. That day had arrived and Papa told me that they would leave me home for some time so I shouldn't be upset. I felt very disappointed and dejected, when I heard this. I was desperately waiting to visit the new place. I thought, "How can Mom do this to me? Will she leave me alone at home? Why did she tell me that all of us would visit a new place?" I thought that I will have to do something but I needed mom's support for that.

The vehicle arrived on the set time, Papa's Personal Security Officer, Boro opened the door for Mom and she took her seat. I also happened to be there, so I instinctively jumped into the vehicle. Mom started patting me and said,

"Sultan, my child, your Papa does not want to take you there but don't worry. I will try my best to help you, just have faith in me." After a few minutes Papa also came and took his seat.

As soon as he saw me sitting in the car, he asked me to get down but I didn't budge. I paid a deaf ear to his instructions. Mom requested Papa to take me also alongwith with them. Papa emphatically said, "NO. Who will take care of him there?" I thought, "Papa, you still don't know that I can be very stubborn if the time requires. After all my name is Sultan, the Emperor." I just turned my face towards the window as if no one was talking to me, no one had the courage to disobey him like this. Before mom could say something but Boro intervened and said, "Sir, I will handle him well. Please don't worry about Sultan." Then Papa relented or maybe it was a face saving device for him because he had clearly seen that I was not in a mood to listen to him at all. He half-heartedly asked Brahmo to bring my leash, I thanked Boro in my heart. Mom had a sweet smile on her face and I thought, "Hurray, I won!"

Brahmo quickly ran inside and brought the leash, Mom kept it inside and we started for the temple. I felt very happy to be a part of this journey as I got an opportunity to see beautiful mountains and lots of greenery. It was amazing, I thought, "Delhi is full of markets, tall buildings and lots of population but Assam is so beautiful." Earlier I used to think that Lodhi Garden was the greenest place in the world but after coming here, my opinion had changed altogether. After a journey of about one and half hour we reached the temple. I was still without the leash, when the vehicle was about to reach, I saw that there were two ice-cream vendors, three or four girls and women, who were selling earthern lamps and flowers. So many goats were also grazing there, I got excited to see so many goats at one place. I wanted to see them from close because their colour was a little different.

When Boro opened the door, I suddenly jumped out of the car and started running towards the goats, I ran like as I had never run before. Even I didn't know that I was capable of running so fast. Seeing me, coming in their direction, the goats started bleating, "Maa, Maa." They ran in different directions to save their lives, the ice-cream vendors and girls had also left their places and started running here and there, there was total chaos. I was surprised, why everybody had started running here and there, after seeing me. Suddenly I heard some familiar voices from a far, "Sultan, stop. Sultan, stop." I was also tired of running so fast, I decided to pay heed to those calls which were asking me to stop. After all, there could be no other better way to save my grace, so I decided to stop.

Later on I came to know that Mom, Papa and Boro were desperately requesting me to stop. I was also very exhausted, I was puffing and panting, I think I had never run such a distance at such a speed so I was feeling very tired. After a few minutes Boro arrived and put the leash on my waist, he brought me in, to my parents. Mom said to me, "Sultan, I knew about your running capabilities very well but I just did not know that you can run so fast, so fast! Simply incredible!" I knew mom, she had always praised me for everything, I did. She would praise me even if I pee or poop but I was very sure that papa would scold me for creating fear amongst the animals and so many human-beings. I thought, "Will he scold me right now in the presence of his staff or later?"

I was feeling very thirsty after running so much, I started panting very badly. Mom immediately understood that I wanted to have water but she had forgotten to bring my bowl. I think she must have got some idea because she asked Boro to get a water bottle from the vehicle. She cupped her palms, then she asked Boro to pour some water in her palms. He poured water into it and I started drinking water from the innovative cup. I think Boro must have poured water for four-five times, my stomach had become full but thirst was not quenched.

The temple was a little far, we had to climb some stairs and we finally reached the temple. My Mom plucked a big leaf from a tree, washed it and shaped it into a bowl and filled water from the tap. She gave me some more water, I drank the water in a few seconds. I was still feeling very thirsty, she again gave me some more water and I finished that also. I had never drunk so much water in such a short time. When I had got some relief, Papa and Mom visited the place and offered their prayers. The Priest gave us some Prasad to eat, it had some pieces of apples. Since Papa knew about my craving for apples so he gave me all the pieces to eat. When the Inspector saw me eating apple, he said, "Sir, I have never seen a dog eating apples. He is really a strange dog. I must say." I thought, "How many dogs have you seen? I am Sultan and I am different. Ha Ha Ha."

After this incidence I was feeling very happy that I was capable of running so fast, I felt very proud of myself, just as my Mom was. I was sure that I will definitely get a scolding from papa. When we were seated in the vehicle, my heart started sinking, when he said to me, "Sultan, you must be thinking that I am going to scold you for scaring so many people. Well if you are thinking that, then you are absolutely wrong. Wow! Sultan today you have given me a surprise because I used to think that you were capable of running only in dreams. Today you had run at the speed of a bullet, I just can't believe this but my eyes have witnessed this. So I have to believe this, I also want to share with you that I had another misconception about you. I also used to think that you don't have qualities of a big dog but today you have defied all my misconceptions. You are definitely a very capable big dog."

I felt proud of myself and thought, "I had never got such an opportunity in Delhi because there was not so much open space for me to run and there were no goats, no lamp sellers to inspire me to run. Of course there were ice-crème sellers but they never got afraid of me. It was such a great achievement for me because I had scared so many people and animals without harming anyone."

It was such an event that I could never forget in my life.

Chapter 69

Brahmputra and I

Papa had to go somewhere for an inspection, so Mom and I were alone at home. I heard her speaking to someone on the phone, saying that she wanted to take me boating in the Brahmaputra River. She asked the person on the phone to book an entire boat for us. I had only heard of rivers until now, so I only thought of a river as a hole in the ground with slightly more water than a pond. Little did I know how big a river actually was, especially one as mighty as the Brahmaputra in Guwahati! I could only imagine myself swimming in the shallow ponds in Lodhi Garden, chasing ducks. I couldn't even imagine what being on a boat would be like, because I'd never been on one before. All I could do to make the wait bearable was tell myself that I would experience these new things soon.

We left the next morning to go to the river and I was very excited the whole ride there. After some time, we reached what Mom said was the river shore. After we got out of the car, we walked towards the booking counter. I waited with Brahmo holding my leash while Rajbongshi went to buy our tickets. As we were waiting, passersby would stare at me as they walked past. So many people were staring at me on their way past that I thought about charging them tickets for dog-watching. We would've been rich!

At last, the wait was over, and Rajbongshi called us over to the shore. We began walking towards the boat, and that's when I caught sight of the river. It was immense! Almost as vast as the forests we had passed during our car ride, but devoid of any trees—just endless water! Compared to this river, the ponds in Lodhi Garden seemed like mere droplets. And our boat was sizable too! While it couldn't match the grandeur of the river, it could easily accommodate twice as many people as we had. There were still passengers on the boat from the previous ride, and they stared intently as they disembarked. It must have been their first time witnessing a dog boarding a boat, just like it was mine.

On her way out, a girl stopped next to me and began petting me.

"What a beautiful dog! How handsome!"

She made me blush. I don't think getting compliments from strangers could ever get old. She left, and two boys came up to us to help us get onto the boat. Once we were all properly seated, a man got in and started the boat. It started making a loud sound, like it was coughing up dust. It scared me a lot, and I ran away from it, towards Mom. When Rajbongshi saw me, he told Mom to take care that I shouldn't jump into the river.

As I calmed down and went to sit next to Mom, she confidently assured him that I wouldn't do such a stupid thing.

"Don't worry about him, he's quite intelligent. He knows how dangerous the river is and why he shouldn't jump into it."

Hearing her reassured me of my own intelligence, but Rajbongshi was still unsure.

"Madam, he's still an animal. He doesn't know the consequences of jumping into the water. Should I come and hold his leash?"

Mom chuckled and started petting me and said, "I think most people suffer from 'Human-Superiority-Syndrome'. They think that because humans are the most intelligent, other animals must lack any basic intellect. That's obviously not the case. God has endowed every creature with the wisdom it needs to survive."

My Mom had always questioned this way of thinking, as had I. Rajbongshi seemed a little embarrassed when he heard her, and didn't raise any questions about my intelligence after that.

Once again, I looked at the river, and it seemed even bigger now. I had never seen this much water in my life! Water stretched out as far as I could see, even beyond the horizon. If I had only lived on the river, I would have believed that the world was all water and no land. It felt stupid to think that Lodhi Garden's ponds were a lot of water. I felt very lucky to have gotten the opportunity to take in the sights. Mom always loved doing fun things that were just for us!

At one point, Rajbongshi pointed towards a small piece of land.

"Madam, can you see that? That's the smallest river island on Earth, Umananda."

I looked where he was pointing, and saw the piece of land. Mom then explained to me what it was.

"Sultan, you probably don't know what an island is, do you? It's land that is surrounded by water on all sides."

She then asked Rajbongshi to take us around the island one time so we could see it up-close. He told the man driving the boat to circle around it, and I realized how small it really was when I saw that it took us less than a minute to circle it.

We came up to a small shore, got down and started walking on the sand. Everything I had seen so far was unbelievably different from what I had seen in Delhi. We spent a few minutes on the shore, looking at white sand and strange shells, and then we got back onto our boat. On our way away from it, I saw some settlements on the island we had just left. Finally, our ride was over and we reached the same place where we had boarded the boat. The ferryman helped us get down, and we went back into the same cabin we had bought tickets from. Throughout our walk, people stared at me in amazement, but I preferred to ignore them. Finally, we reached our car, after getting in, we left to go back home. I was in a great mood the whole time, having experienced a river view and a boat ride for the first time in my life.

There were so many places worth seeing in Assam! I knew I was very fortunate to experience all the things I had gotten to experience, because hardly any dogs from Delhi got to see a river like the Brahmaputra and have a boat ride in it. It widened my mental horizons.

Chapter 70

A Visit to Pandu Port

One day, when Papa was gone for an official tour, Mom made another plan to explore Guwahati. This time, Rajbongshi had planned to take us to a new place. Mom told me the plan.

"Sultan, tomorrow we're going to see a port named Pandu Port. A port is a place on the shore of a sea or a river, where people can stand and get on and off boats. Rajbongshi told me it was an important port where a lot of trading used to take place."

Mom had explained a lot of things to me, but most of them went over my head. I was just happy to go see something new and exciting again.

We set out for Pandu Port the next morning. We had to drive through crowded lanes and markets, and eventually we reached the entrance gate to the port. Brahmo took a hold of my leash and we got out of the car to walk through the entrance gate. We reached a wide open area with a barricaded gate. I was told that this port was built on the Brahmaputra. I then saw a huge boat with many, many floors, and remembered Mom telling me that a boat that big is called a ship. It had a lot of people walking around on it like it was a road!

On the other side of the ship, I could see a huge and majestic bridge. Rajbongshi told Mom that it was built after a

Chinese invasion in 1962, and that the Chinese forces had managed to advance until the area where the bridge began. He said that after the war, the government of India built this bridge to connect Assam to the rest of India. I understood then that this bridge was very important.

He then told Mom that trade used to be carried out from this port, but it had now stopped. He also showed her railway tracks on the bridge, on which trains travelled and carried goods. The tracks now looked abandoned. I wondered how busy this place must have been in the past, and it seemed sad to see it looking so lonely and abandoned now. Its condition was quite pathetic. We spent another hour there, and then we got back in the car and went home.

Every outing I had had in Guwahati had shown and taught me new things. It felt like I was exploring an entirely new world. I couldn't wait to see what I would learn next!

Chapter 71

A Small Separation and a Pleasant Surprise

After many days had passed, Mom said to me,"Sultan, I have to go to Delhi for some urgent work. I won't stay there for many days but I would come back with a pleasant surprise for you. Till then keep guessing." After a few days, I saw, Mom was packing her luggage, I understood that she was going to Delhi. I became sad that she was going to leave me. Though she always used tell me clearly, if my family would be preparing for any vacation. I liked this honesty, this would give me some time to mentally prepare myself and it used to become easier for me to cope up with the separations.

Despite having this satisfaction, I had become sad to know that I will have to stay away from mom for a few days. Actually I could never imagine my life without her, right from my first day in the family, I had spent every day with mom. She always took care of my smallest needs and moreover she was the one, who had never left me alone. Next day she got ready in the morning and played her favourite Assamese song, before leaving, she kissed me and said, "Do not worry, Sultan. I will be back soon." Then Papa went to drop her at the airport. I was alone at home and I kept sitting near the door with a sad heart till Papa came back.

Life had become very lifeless without Mom, as Papa used to be in his office. Though whenever he would come back, he used to shower all his love on me. He had also started coming back a little earlier from the office. His efforts wouldn't suffice to fill the vaccum that mom's absence had created. I had become used to see Mom everyday, every moment, I was missing Mom terribly. I didn't know when she would come back so I used to eagerly wait for her.

One fine day Papa said to me that he had to go to the airport. I immediately understood that he was going to pick up Mom from the airport but what was the pleasant surprise that she would give me? I was sitting in the open verandah and waiting for my parents. After a long wait, the vehicle reached near the verandah, I immediately got up, door of the vehicle was opened. My heart started beating fast, imagination at the top and eyes on the vehicle, without blinking my eyelids. First papa got down followed by Mom, then the pleasant surprise. I thought, "Oh wow! Garima, she is not merely a pleasant surprise but very very pleasant surprise. Indeed!" When I saw her, I started dancing, my heart started dancing. In fact every part of my body was dancing with immense joy. I just didn't know that how I should express my feelings, how I could tell her that I was very happy that day.

I felt more happy, when I saw that Garima had brought a beautiful toy for me, she said to me, "It is a teddy bear for you. If I press this button, you will hear Christmas song, jingle bell jingle bell. This is the gift sent for you by Oscar, a pet dog, I take care of him whenever I have free time. You know that Oscar is very fond of me. Whenever I have free time I do dog-sitting with Oscar. Sultan, I am paid for that, I don't like this but Oscar's parents insist on paying me." Though she was talking to me but all my attention was fixed on the toy she had brought for me. I liked playing with the soft toy especially when it played Christmas song. Garima had also brought very nice eatables for me from there, I had never tasted such super tasty stuff earlier.

Now my life had become eventful as Garima and Mom used to take me for a walk in the morning around 9 AM. We used to come back after 40 minutes. Again they used to take me out in the evening. Mom had made friends with a group of ladies, who used to come at the same time for their evening walk. Whenever we would cross them, they used to get scared of me. Though Mom used to assure them that I would never bite anyone but this assurance couldn't alleviate their fear. One of them said to mom that I looked very ferocious. How I could tell them I was very gentle my nature. I thought, "Perhaps my jet black colour and my size made people scared of me. How could I assure them of my peaceful nature?"

One day, when we were taking evening walk in the Railway Club, a young female puppy appeared and started playing with me. I liked it very much and I was happy to get a dog's company. I had hardly seen any street dog in the Railway colony, so she was just like a boon for me. She started following us and entered our house with us. She was very naughty and I also liked playing with her. When it was dark she went back to the club. Next day, when we were out for a morning walk, she again appeared and started licking my ears. I also responded in the same affectionate manner. She must be three to four months old so she was full of energy. She was so playful that she had started disturbing me when I was peeing. She did not let me relieve myself fully so I got very irritated and felt that her company had started bothering me a lot.

When Mom saw this she tried to shoo her away but she kept following me. Brahmo showed her the stick, so she got scared but she didn't stop following us. She went to the other side of the road, just like the previous day, she entered our house from a hole in the hedge. The sentry didn't come to know of this, we got a surprise when she suddenly appeared before us. That evening she didn't leave our house and preferred to stay in our house only. When Mom saw this, she got worried for her safety from leopard. Brahmo and Mom kept her in the covered verandah, which was fully safe as it had iron door and strong iron railing.

Since she was a street dog, she was habitual of sleeping in the open so she started crying. Maybe, she was feeling that she had been jailed. Papa got angry when he heard her crying because he thought that it was a bad omen. He wanted the puppy to be dropped back immediately. Mom and Brahmo were worried for her life so they decided to leave her to the Railway Club premises. So Brahmo took her and dropped her there, this is how we got some relief. We had hardly imagined that our relief was so shortlived because she appeared again in the morning. When Mom saw her affection for our family she decided to let her stay during the day time but I was not at all happy with this decision because she was a real trouble for me. She used to follow me everywhere and used to lick me unnecessarily.

She really had started bothering me a lot, especially, when I would be peeing or pooping. Now I was fed up of her company and wanted to get rid of her, enough of that, I had played with her! She had become like a pestering housefly for me, the more I would try to run away from her, the more she used to hover on me. One day she crossed her limits, when she had bitten Garima on her leg when she was enjoying her swings on a hammock. I got very sad to see that she fell down from the hammock out of sudden shock. I thought, "How could that puppy bite someone from my family? How dare she?

I was shocked when I heard that Mom ----- my Mom, gave her a name, Toffee, just like she gave me a name. I shuddered to see this and thought, "Is she going to raise her the same way she has raised me? Will she give her also a bath as she has always been giving me? Will the family keep her also with them? Will they give her all the love which I had always got? No, No, No." Though I was becoming apprehensive but I knew very well somewhere in the heart of my heart, that my family could never give the same treatment that it gave me, to some other dog.

I couldn't take it anymore, I think I was becoming possessive and jealous. Perhaps, yes, but I couldn't help it. I got some respite, when I heard mom's conversation with Brahmo. She said to him, "We could have raised Toffee also if we were going to stay here for some more time only. I can allow her to live here for as many days as she wants but she will have to always remain outside the house. She would never be allowed to enter the house. Brahmo, we also have to think about her safety from the leopard. Do you have any idea to protect her?" she took a pause and continued, "What if we should shift her near the barrocks. She will be safe there as there is no threat of leopard. I will keep sending the food for her." Then Mom discussed the matter with Papa and

Garima both, a unanimous decision was taken that Toffee should be shifted near Police Barrocks where she would be safe and will be fed by our constables. I was so relieved to hear that. At last I was going to get rid of her, she would be shifted away from me and my family.

Though it was bothering all of us that a puppy will be displaced from her natural habitat but my family was of the opinion that life was more important than habitat. Next day we bid farewell to Toffee, suddenly my anger against her vanished in a second. Though Mom was sending her off but she was feeling sorry for her. Out of love she also sent food for her. Finally Rajbongnshi took her to drop her near the barrocks, he came back after some time and reported that she was successfully dropped and he had given her food also. Everyday Mom used to take news about her welfare, after a few days Sunil told her that Toffee had mixed up well with other street dogs and was peacefully living there. All of us were so relieved to hear that Toffee was happy, safe and sound.

This is how Toffee's chapter closed from our lives, with her happiness and safety.

Chapter 72

Goldie and the Leopard

It was a lazy Sunday morning. I was sitting next to Garima on the sofa while Mom and Papa were enjoying their morning tea. The silence broke when Mom talked to Papa.

"I was in the kitchen yesterday, and I found five small bowls of the same size. I know they're not for Sultan, so whose are they?"

"Well, it's Sunday...", Papa said.

"I don't have to go to work and I have plenty of time. Do you want to listen to a long story?"

Garima and Mom looked at him and anxiously said yes.

"We've become animal lovers ever since Sultan came into our lives, especially when it comes to dogs. When I first got this big bungalow, a female dog started coming up to the front of our house with four puppies. I was always happy to see them, and I named the mother 'Goldie' because she had white fur and golden-blonde spots on her back. I had asked the staff to take care of them, and we'd give them bread and milk twice a day. Brahmo decided to go and buy five bowls for all of them. I'd started playing with them, too. Maybe I was missing Sultan, so I decided to give shelter to them."

Garima and Mom continued to look at him intensely, fully engrossed in the story. Papa continued.

"It was peak monsoon season, so it rained and thundered heavily almost every day. One night, when the sky was really dark, the thunder got louder and louder. It sounded like the sky was going to rip apart and flood the earth. The electricity took a hit, which only made it seem worse. The thunder was so deafeningly loud that even I was unsettled, so I can only imagine how terrified Goldie must have been, in the eerie darkness. Even though it was dark, she must have figured out that something was stalking her and approaching her, and she started barking desperately. She must have tried to cover her four puppies, but the leopards that live around these parts pounced on one of her puppies and took it away. By the time one of our sentries had arrived to help her, the leopards had already disappeared."

Papa took a deep breath, and continued.

"She couldn't protect all her children. When I woke up the next morning and went outside, Goldie came up to me and started pulling at my *kurta,* trying to take me in the direction where the leopard had taken her beloved child. She was whining and crying the whole time. I couldn't understand anything at first, but it became clear that she was trying to convey something. I became suspicious and remembered the barking I had heard the previous night, so I found her puppies and counted them. It was shocking when I realized there were only three now. I understood that the leopard had come down and devoured one puppy. I tried to console her to no avail. A couple of days later, she left our house and took her children away, probably to some safer place. She looked so sad and defeated… it took me many days to forget that whole episode."

Hearing Papa talk about this made me scared of the leopards, too. It made me understand why Papa had made strict guidelines about not taking me out after sunset, and why Mom would send people with big sticks to accompany me whenever it got dark.

It also made sense why Mom had moved Toffee away from our house to a safer and more crowded place. I finally understood why she had to leave, even though she wasn't comfortable not sleeping in an open area. She wasn't safe out in the open, after all.

One morning, when I was out on the front lawn, I saw a strange dog approach our house. I started barking at it to get it to go away, but Papa walked up to me and asked me to stop. The dog had gotten so scared by my barking that it immediately ran away. Papa looked like he felt bad for the dog, and Mom came out to ask what was going on.

"Goldie had come to see me, but Sultan barked at her and scared her, so she ran away." He continued.

"Goldie herself was a victim of the leopard's attacks. She was lucky that she survived. Some kind people reached her just in time to take her to a hospital, and she had to get twenty stitches on her back, but her life was saved."

After hearing this, I regretted my actions and decided not to bark at her ever again. It reminded me of the dangers posed by leopards. This place is beautiful, but full of threats I never had to worry about in Delhi.

Chapter 73

The Badminton Court and My Mischiefs

Our new bungalow was so huge that Papa had made a badminton court in it. When Mom and Garima had arrived in Guwahati, he had the court cleaned up and a new net was tied up. Papa was very keen to play badminton with both of them, but Mom had some problem that kept her from playing, so it became routine for Papa and Garima to play badminton in the mornings. Mom used to sit by the side and judge them. Whenever I saw the shuttle move from one side to the other, I got excited. I wanted to catch it in my mouth, so I would run in to pick the shuttle up and chew on it. I had managed to capture many shuttles, but Papa and Garima didn't seem to appreciate it. They would always ask Mom to take me into the house and keep me occupied. Initially, Mom did this very sincerely and kept me engaged so Papa and Garima could play badminton with no interruptions. Eventually, however, I started missing chasing and playing with the shuttle. I thought that I wouldn't get to play with the shuttle anymore… little did I know that Mom was planning some mischief.

One morning when Garima and Papa were playing, Mom opened the door and signaled to me to go out and play. I ran out and found the shuttle, grabbed it, took it to the front lawn and chewed it up to my heart's content. Papa and Garima ran to me to find out what was going on, and they were both confused as to how I had come out of the house. Mom started acting clueless and regretful. Papa tried to convince her that it was just a mistake, but perhaps Garima saw through it. She confidently claimed that she knew Mom better than Papa did, and that she had let me out on purpose. Papa tried to reason with her, but she couldn't be convinced.

From that day onwards, Mom started playing this game more often. One every two or three days, she would secretly open the door for me to let me go at the shuttle and hunt it like it were prey. Then, when I was found out, she would make a sorry face and act regretful. I started enjoying her acting, but Mom and I were unaware that Papa was starting to become suspicious of us. We didn't realize that he had started keeping an eye on us…

One fine day, Papa circled around the house and entered from the back to catch Mom opening the door. Right as Mom opened the door and told me to go and get the shuttle, she realized that Papa was standing right behind her. When she turned around, she was horrified to see that she had been caught. There was an embarrassed expression on her face, but she didn't try to defend herself. I, meanwhile, arrived at the front lawn only to see Garima already holding up the shuttle. Papa then went outside to join her.

"You were right, Garima. While we were playing badminton, your mom was busy playing games with us. She deliberately let Sultan out so he could spoil our game. I've asked Brahmo to keep Sultan in the kitchen, so we can finally play without interruptions."

And so my shuttle hunts came to an end and Mom came to immerse herself in newspapers every morning.

Chapter 74

We Travelled in a Saloon

One day, Papa was talking to Mom and Garima about having to go somewhere.

"I have to go to Darjeeling soon, to conduct an inspection. I'll come back after two or three days."

Mom immediately said that if he was going to Darjeeling, the rest of us would accompany him as well.

"Oh, and don't worry about Sultan, because he will join us, too. All of us are going to go visit Darjeeling!"

Garima expressed her excitement, saying that she had never gotten the chance to visit Darjeeling because of how far it was from Delhi. Papa didn't get the chance to get a word amidst the chaos, and so the decision was made final. I was happy to get the chance to visit a new place again. Once the excitement had settled, Papa announced the plan.

"We will set out two days from now. Make sure to pack for three days."

After giving instructions, he left to go to the office. Mom and Garima started making plans for the trip. I, too, couldn't help but get excited. Somehow, two days passed by quickly, and soon we were on our way to the Kamakhya Railway Station to board our train. The train must have been running late, so Papa asked the three of us to sit in the waiting room for some time. Time felt like it slowed to a crawl, and waiting was starting to become unbearable. Suddenly, the doors of the waiting room swung open and a man came in. He started picking up our luggage, and I stood up because I thought that we might be getting robbed. Before I could make a move, he told us that the train had arrived. I looked at Mom and Garima, and they looked happy and relieved. All of us stood up and followed the man to the train platform.

We arrived at a coach and saw Papa already there, waiting for us. He helped me board the coach. When I got up and entered, I looked around to see that this train was quite different from the interior of the Rajdhani Express. There was a beautiful sofa on one side and a dining table on the other. It looked so grand that even the Rajdhani Express couldn't hold a candle to it.

Soon after, Garima and Mom entered the train. There were two beds with beautiful blankets beyond the sofa on both sides of the wall. Mom seemed to have noticed that I was observing everything and was a little confused.

"Sultan, this kind of coach is called a saloon. When very senior officers go somewhere on official visits, they get to use this facility. There are two bedrooms with attached bathrooms. Your Papa and I will use that bedroom over there, and you and Garima will use the other one. There's even a cook here who will make our food, and I've asked him to make plain boiled chicken for you."

She asked Garima to show me the bathroom. Garima came to me and took me there. She opened the door, and I was surprised to see a very neat and clean bathroom. By now, I had stopped feeling like the proud son of a proud father, because I knew that I would get many chances to experience that feeling.

Some time passed, and a person came in to tell us that our dinner was ready. Papa asked us to go to the dining room. Mom went and brought my bowl and stand. Then we went to the dining room and she asked the cook to bring my chicken. Once I had started eating, he laid the table and my family began to eat as well. When we were all done, we went back to the rooms. Garima picked up her bag and mine, and we went to our bedroom. Since it had been a long day and we were very tired, Garima turned off the light and asked me to go to sleep. The gentle movement of the train made it so when I closed my eyes, it felt like I was on a swing. I started feeling sleepy, and soon I dozed off.

Both of us woke up the next morning when we heard Mom's voice at the door. She knocked and asked Garima to wake up.

"Garima, Sultan, it's time to wake up. It's nine in the morning. The train has stopped for twenty minutes, so your Papa wants to take Sultan for a walk."

Upon hearing what Mom said, Garima immediately got up and opened the door. I quickly ran out and found Papa, and we went for our walk so I could fully relieve myself. When we came back to the coach, I found that Mom had already prepared my breakfast.

The train had started moving again, and I was now finding it difficult to maintain my balance. I somehow managed to finish my food. In the meantime, Garima came out of the bedroom to join us and Papa welcomed her.

"Good morning! You're finally here. We were waiting for you to come eat breakfast. Let's sit next to the window and enjoy our food."

Papa asked the cook to keep our food next to the window shelf. He got up, and we all followed him to one end of the coach, where there was a very big glass window.

"What an amazing view!", Garima remarked.

"With a view like this, the food will taste even better."

Everyone sat down as the cook began to bring their food to them. When everyone was finished eating, I thought that we would all go back into our rooms, but I was surprised to see that everyone just sat there. We spent some time near that window and enjoyed the outside view. After some time passed, Papa told us that the train would soon arrive at our station, and that everyone should go to their rooms to pack up their luggage. Soon, the train stopped and we got down. We had to walk to get outside the train station, and we reached a big vehicle. Papa asked us to get in, and everyone entered with their luggage. Once everyone was inside and all the luggage was put in the back, the car started. I was so excited to see where we would arrive!

Chapter 75

A Visit to Darjeeling

Papa told us that we would arrive at our destination at around lunchtime, and that we would use the vehicle we were in throughout our stay in Darjeeling. After many hours, the car finally stopped near a beautiful building. Papa asked us to get out, and our luggage was taken into the building. We started walking towards the building and once we were inside, a man at a counter asked Papa to write something on a register. As he was writing, Boro came up to us and asked us to enter a lift. By the time we were in the lift, Papa joined us with keys in his hands. We rode the lift up and reached our room. Everyone got out and started unpacking. Mom unpacked my bag first and quickly took out my winter coat. I was quite eager to wear the coat, because I had never felt as cold in Delhi as I did here. Papa put my coat on me and asked Boro to take me outside for a walk. He did as he was told, and we went for a walk. Once I had relieved myself, Boro brought me back inside. I was glad to be indoors again, because it was terribly cold outside.

Mom asked the chef to prepare food for all of us. We all sat on a dining table and Papa switched on a heater, which made the room much more cozy. After some time, the cook brought out our food. Mom gave me my meal first, and then everyone else began eating their lunch.

Once again, Garima and I were sharing a room. Garima asked me to come up to the bed because of how cold the marble floor was. She wrapped me and herself in a warm blanket, and since we had had a tiring journey, both of us soon fell asleep.

The next day, we went outside and started exploring. Darjeeling was the first place where I had seen high and mighty mountains. Some of them looked to be covered in snow. From where I stood, the mountains went up so high that they seemed to touch the sky! It was very exciting to see something so awesome. As we were admiring the mountains, Mom walked up to us and told us that we were going to go boating. As we were getting in the car, Mom showed me some beautiful tea gardens.

We stayed in Darjeeling for two days, and our stay was very enjoyable. After two days, however, we had to undertake a long and arduous journey. After a really long time, we finally reached a small town. Papa asked us to stay at a rest house while he completed his inspection, and to have lunch without him. We did as he said and went to a resthouse. Mom served me food and Boro then took me for a walk. When I came back, Mom and Garima started having their lunch. Papa joined us after a long time, hurriedly ate his lunch and asked us to get ready. He told us that we had to leave soon to make it in time to board our train back home. Once he was done eating, we quickly got in the car and eventually reached the station.

After walking to our platform and boarding the train, I immediately recognized the sofa and dining table I saw. I knew right then that we were going to travel in the same saloon as before, which was great news to me. Everyone else entered, and Boro walked in with a white plastic bag in hand, which he carefully put down on the dining table. He then said his goodbyes, everyone thanked him, and he left. Some time after the train had started and everyone was settled, Mom pulled a box out of the plastic bag on the dining table. She opened the box and inside was a cake! It turned out that today was Garima's birthday. We celebrated her birthday in the saloon itself.

After an enjoyable ride in the saloon, we finally got back home. The journey was very memorable, and the saloon ride had made my trip unforgettable.

Chapter 76

One More Separation

After one and half a month I saw both Garima and Mom packing their luggage so I immediately understood that they were going back to Delhi. Mom had started telling me about three-four days in advance. After three-four days, they said bye and hugged me. Mom said, "Sultan, we are leaving for Dellhi and soon we will meet there. Bye, my child." In response to this I wagged my tail though I didn't want to show any kind of happiness but it happened instinctively. I knew that now I will have to live there alone. Papa will be busy in his office and I will be alone at our home, with Brahmo and Kumar. How sad! After I had said bye, Brahmo picked up their luggage and kept it in the vehicle and then all my family members also sat down in the vehicle.

I saw Garima and Mom waved their hands to me, I also said bye to them in my heart and conveyed it through my bark. Papa came back after two hours and showered all his love on me and promised me that he will try his best to give me as much time as possible. He also said, "Sultan, I can not give the love and care that you have got from both Garima and your Mom but I will try to maximum time possible. I will try to come back from office as soon as possible." I was so happy to hear that my Papa was so caring and loving.

It was getting hotter in Assam now and I wanted to have a bath, moreover my Sunday bath was due. I was thinking that I will have to remain without getting a bath. I was surprised when I heard Papa asking Brahmo to prepare neem water for my bath. Now Papa was going to give me a bath, how nice! I was feeling that I was very fortunate to get a bath by Papa for the first time in my life. Brahmo helped him in bathing me. When the bath was over, I got boiled egg as a treat. I thought, "Papa is trying his best to give me the same treatment that I had been getting from Mom. I really appreciated his effort and thanked him immensely." He had started giving me more time in the absence of Mom, he had started coming back from the office a bit early. Brahmo was always at my service, taking care of all my needs.

Though I was absolutely comfortable but I was missing Mom because I had never spent a day without her, I just wanted to be with her as soon as possible.

Chapter 77

I came back to Delhi

After many days had passed, Papa told me that soon I would join Mom at Delhi. He also told me that I would go back with Dobi and Satish. On the assigned day, he sent me back to Delhi by Rajdhani Express. During the train journey, I came to know through them that Papa had vacated the bunglow and shifted to a guest house. Then I understood that why he had sent me back to Delhi, maybe it would have been difficult for me to live in one room apartment. It was a long and boring journey with Dobi and Satish, they were just talking to each other only whereas Mom had been talking to me during the whole journey.

After a long journey finally we reached Delhi and to my surprise Mom was there at the station to welcome me with a garland and rose petals. She put the garland round my neck and started showering petals at me and people gathered there to see me, I think they must be wondering at such a unique welcome of a dog. Though it was very difficult for me to keep wearing that garland because the flowers had a strong smell but still I kept wearing that. I didn't want to hurt Mom's emotions so I didn't resist at all. When we were seated in our car, she removed that garland, to my rellief.

After a few minutes journey, we reached our colony then we entered the lift and reached our home. Mahinder was there to welcome me, he gave me a tight hug. His hug was revealing that how much he had missed me. Then Meena also came and hugged me in such a manner that it conveyed his love and emotions for me. I was overwhelmed to get such a welcome from both of them, I was wondering that a mere hug could also convey all the feelings. This could definitely not be expressed through words, a simple touch could convey everything when the words would fail. Mahinder had prepared chicken for me for the dinner which I relished too much, I think that his preparation had also conveyed his feelings for me.

After having my food, I wanted to take rest because the journey was very long and hectic. Meena had already switched on the A.C. of the room, so it had become very cozy. Mom and I entered the room, Mom sat on the bed and I laid down myself on the floor and soon I was fast asleep. I think that I must have slept for a long time.

When I got up, I saw that Mom and Meena were sitting in the living room so I also joined them. When Mom saw me, she said, "I hope you are fresh now after a long sleep. Come, my child, sit by my side." I quickly jumped on the sofa and she started caressing me lovingly. Then she said to Meena, "Meena, you know Sultan has changed my thoughts and views completely." Meena became curious and asked, "Madam, how has Sultan changed your views?"

Mom replied, "Meena, we human beings have made many scientific achievements. We have got mobile, T.V. A.C., heater and cars etc. All these things make our lives comfortable, whereas animals were naked and are still naked. We call ourselves intelligent but do you know that Sultan is smarter than us. He not only understands Hindi and

English but our gestures also. But have we been able to understand his language yet? No." "Definitely, no." She continued.

Then Mom said, "Meena, we've so much progress but we don't have intuitive minds like dogs have. Sir had told me this long ago, I was quite surprised to listen to that. You know that my in-laws live in a village on Indo-Pak border. Suddenly the street dogs, there, started crying severely, while keeping their face on Pakistan's side. Elders of the village took it as a bad omen so everyone tried to dissuade the dogs but to no avail. This continued for five-six days and you know, Meena, exactly after six days, Pakistan declared war on India and heavy shelling started from their side. Many people lost their lives in that firing. Now, tell me Meena, did the dogs have an intuition about this, could they sense that such a casualty was going to take place? If yes, it would mean that dogs could see the near future. Haven't so many dogs saved their parent's life by sensing some danger in the near future. I have read so many times that the pet didn't allow his parent to travel by plane, which was going to crash. Despite having so much advancements, have we been able to develop this quality?"

After listening to this Meena said that he fully agreed with her. After his approval Mom continued, "Meena, you know all the children are the same, when Madhav and Garima were infants, they always wanted my lap, same was with Sultan. You have seen how he always used to sit on my lap always. So where is the difference? Meena, I have subscribed to one spiritual chanell, according to one spiritual leader, there are different Gods for the animals and human beings. Meena, do you think that there are different

God for animals and different one for human beings?" Meena emphatically said, "Madam, there is only one God for all the species. How could spiritual leader give such an irresponsible statement."

Mom continued, "Earlier, I also used to suffer from Human- Supiriority -Syndrom and used to consider animals as inferior to human beings but now I have changed my opinion. I feel animals are spiritually more evolved because animals don't cheat, don't kill others for just a few rupees. If animals kill other animals, they do it out of their hunger not out greed or revenge. Some human beings have become so low that they rape girls, they don't even spare minors and commit brutalities on them, no animal would do that. I think that no animals are barbaric but some human beings are definitely barbaric. In animal kingdom, everything takes place with consent. So it is my firm faith that animals are spiritually superior to some human beings. Just like we've a term humanitarian, I would say that all the animals are animaltarian. "

"They don't cheat, no thefts, they don't stab at one's back. They don't cheat their friends, they don't declare war on another pack, they just drive out another pack from their territory. Whereas countries declare war on another country and so many human lives are lost in the war." She continued.

Meena had become speechless and looked mesmerised with what Mom had just said. He said, "Madam, I had never thought from this point of view. You are absolutely right and very convincing. Your views have changed my thoughts also. You have compelled me to start thinking afresh. Please continue and enlighten me more." Mom smiled and said,

"This is all for today, I have to leave for Gurgaon early in the morning."

I was quite surprised and happy to know that Mom took animals in such a high esteem, her thoughts had really impressed me. Her views made me feel very confident of myself and other animals also.

Chapter 78

Gurgaon- Our New House

The next day, Mom was getting ready to go to Gurgaon. She had asked Meena to stay at home with me, and to start packing everything that we didn't need urgently. I was told that we were soon going to shift to a new house in Gurgaon. After having her breakfast, she left with Mahinder for Gurgaon. She then came back home late in the evening. This routine would continue for many days, where she would leave to go to Gurgaon in the morning and come back home at night.

Finally, the day arrived when we started moving to Gurgaon for real. Mom and I were sitting in our car, and Meena and Mahinder were sitting in the truck that was carrying our luggage. After about an hour, we reached our destination. Unlike our previous colony, this place seemed very peaceful and quiet. It was not at all crowded like our Panchkuian colony. There was a tailor sitting on the pavement and one vegetable seller. Besides them we couldn't see anyone. There was no traffic, so no traffic noise and honking horns. It also seemed less polluted unlike Delhi. Mom and I went into our flat right after arriving, with Meena and Mahinder following us much later. Once they came into the flat, they started helping with unloading and unpacking our things, setting things as and where Mom asked. Once most of our things had been unpacked and put up, they made food for us and left.

They came back the next morning, made breakfast for us and started cleaning and setting up the house. Suddenly, I heard a strange loud sound. I got up, wondering what it was, and I realized it was just how the bell sounded in this house when I saw Meena walk to the door. He opened the door, and the person outside said they wanted to see Mom, so Mom went to the door to meet him. When Mom got to the door, he introduced himself.

"Madam, my name is Paswan. I saw that you have a dog with you, and I wanted to let you know that if you need anyone to walk him then I will be glad to offer my services. You can pay me whatever you deem fit."

Mom seemed very happy to hear him say that, and made her offer. "My husband is the one who walks him, and he will come after three days. You will have to take Sultan, my dog, for a walk three times a day until my husband returns, and after that it will be twice a day. I can pay you a thousand rupees per month."

I don't think Paswan was expecting to get paid that much, because he looked very happy to hear Mom's offer and instantly accepted.

I felt happy to hear Mom say that Papa would be joining us soon because I was already missing him a lot. Looking around the house, Mahinder and Meena were still setting things up, but the house had started to take some shape. It became routine for both of them to show up in the morning, continue setting things up and leave in the afternoon, preparing meals for us at both times of the day. Three days passed rather quickly amidst the chaos, and finally Papa came to our new house. When I saw him, I immediately rushed towards him. He hugged me, picked me up and said that he had finally come back to live with his family forever. "I have retired, and now all my time is for my family only."

He then took a round of our new flat and seemed happy to see the progress, praising Mahinder and Meena for their efforts.

Once everything was in order, Mahinder and Meena told Mom that they had been asked to start with their duties at a new place, and that they would do so soon. They said that it would be difficult to stay in a place without me, and thanked Mom for treating them with kindness and respect, saying that they would never forget her.

"I understand. I wish you the best at your new place of work. I won't forget the invaluable service you have given us either."

And so both Mahinder and Meena, after showing me plenty of love and attention on their last day, ended their routine and stopped coming to our new home.

It was clear that a new chapter had started in our lives.

Chapter 79

Our New Attendants

Now that Mahinder and Meena had stopped coming to our house, Mom employed a young woman named Guddi as our domestic help. She was very polite and obedient, and would do all the chores quietly. She was so quiet, in fact, that it was difficult to sense her presence in the house. She would help Mom with all kinds of chores, even when it came to giving me a bath.

One day, when Guddi and Mom were giving me a bath, Guddi started talking to Mom about her dog.

"Our dog, Moti, was very intelligent. We used to loosely tie a bag with a list and some cash around his neck, and he would go and get our groceries. He would even act as a guide dog for my aunt! When she had to go to the bathroom, he would put her stick in his mouth and walk her to it."

She then talked about how Moti would get drunk!

"My husband used to drink a lot, and he would give Moti some alcohol, too. Whenever he would get hungover, he would throw up. I had to clean up the mess, but I never felt bad about it. One day, he just went missing. We looked for him everywhere, but couldn't find him. It was then that we realized that somebody had stolen Moti. He was only with us for a few years, but I still miss him."

I enjoyed hearing Moti's story. It would have been nice to be of service and fetch things for my family, but Papa never gave me that opportunity. Still, I was amazed to see Guddi's love for her dog, even after he had been missing for so long. After the bath, Mom wiped me down and I was given lunch, which I quickly scarfed down. I was already at the door before the doorbell rang. Once it did, Paswan opened the door and walked in. After he put my leash on, we left for our walk. When we were walking around, he started talking to me.

"Sultan, I know you're new here, so I will show you around."

He took me to many lush green places, telling me where we were now, and I thoroughly enjoyed our walk.

On our way back home, he told me that he had liked me the moment he met me.

"I work in this society as a maintenance worker, but I also do odd jobs on the side. When I met you, you seemed so cute and gentle. I decided then that I would offer my service to your parents."

It was nice to walk back home after such a pleasant conversation.

Every day, Paswan would take me for my walks. On one unusual day, he was not walking right, stumbling and almost tripping on things. It turned out that he was drunk! On our way back home, a patrolling police jeep came up to us. A policeman walked out with a tool that looked kind of like a whistle, and asked Paswan to put it in his mouth and breathe. He then looked at it, and asked Paswan to sit in the jeep with me. We got in, and they took us to the police station. One we had arrived, they asked us to get out. Paswan looked like he was very nervous, but I felt fine. I had been around uniformed men since my childhood, so this was nothing new to me.

The inspector started sternly asking Paswan questions about me.

"Sir, he is an Inspector General's dog... his name is Sultan."

After hearing this, he asked the people who had picked us up to drop us off back where they found us. By the time we were back near home, Paswan seemed to have sobered up, and he brought me back home safely.

Chapter 80

Some Disliked My Presence

After shifting to Gurgaon, an entirely new routine had started for all of us. Mom and Guddi had started taking me for small walks in the society's park. Since we were on the sixth floor, we always had to use the lift. Usually it would be just the three of us in the lift but one day, when the lift arrived at our floor, there was already an old man inside. The moment he saw me he said to Mom, "You are like a daughter to me, so I am advising you to abandon your dog immediately. Dog licks and bites are both harmful for human beings (kutte ka kaataa aur kutte ka chata. Dono hi kharab hai.) Listen to my advice and abandon your dog, they are not good for humans."

I thought, "I have been licking all of my family members since I was a child but I never caused them any harm. I wonder what kind of misconceptions some people harbour? What kind of baseless accusations do they make about us?"

When we were in the park, Guddi politely asked Mom, "Madam, that man spoke so much against dogs. You know about my love for Moti and Sultan and I know about your dedication for Sultan, despite that you didn't try to defend dogs..."

I, too, wondered why Mom didn't defend me. She took a deep breath and quietly said, "Guddi, I can not fight every insane person. I have no answer for their misconceptions. I know I can't change their opinion, so I keep quiet. It's as simple as that." I looked at Guddi and found that she was seemed content with Mom's reply.

On another day, when we were going down by the lift, another old man was already in it. He asked Mom not to bring me in, but Mom didn't listen to him. That old man said, "What kind of woman are you? I asked you not to bring the dog inside the lift but you brought him inside anyway." Mom told him that I was harmless because I had never bitten anyone. The man said, "It is a dog and you can never trust an animal. You never know when the animal will change its behaviour." After hearing this Mom replied, "Sir, animals can be truly trusted. If a dog is in the habit of biting, it will always bite. If a dog has never bitten anyone, it never will".

When the man heard this he became furious and said, "Your behaviour shows what kind of family you belong to. Your parents have not taught you any values, I think they must be just like you. The only thing they have taught you is how to disrespect an old man. I had asked you not to bring your dog in, and you did the opposite." Mom was absolutely quiet, but I felt very agitated over his words. Maybe she had realised that it was pointless to argue with that old man. After a few seconds, I, too, started feeling that way and all my anger vanished.

There were many people who would maintain their distance from me the moment they would see me. Some people even used to look at me with disgust. Initially, I used to get very upset over this but gradually I just got used to it. It was difficult for me at first because I had never gotten this kind of treatment in our Panchkuian Road Colony. Mom's attitude that we don't need to respond to an insane person's opinion helped me a lot in dealing with this.

Though I had come out of this to a great extent, I had hardly anticipated that a big problem was looming around the corner. It was a problem that would shake up me and my family thoroughly.

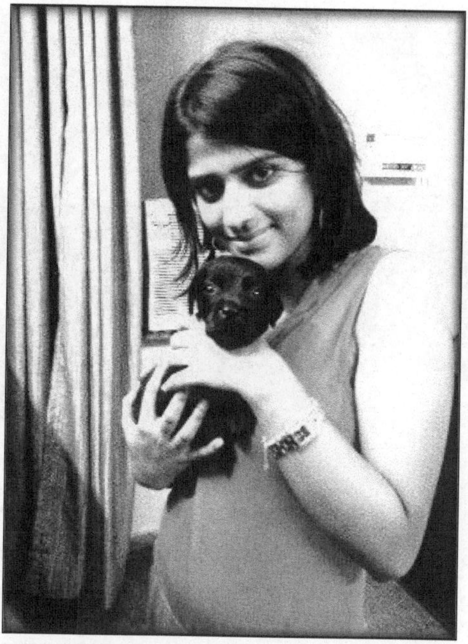

Sultan, two days after his arrival.

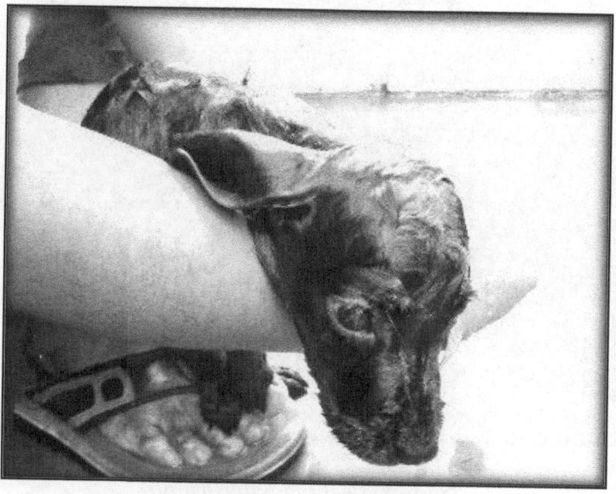

Sultan's first bath

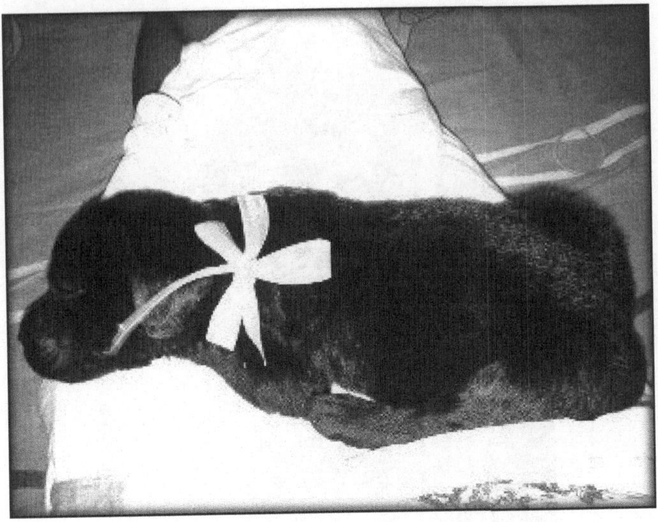

Sultan wearing a ghungroo, tied with chinese ribbon

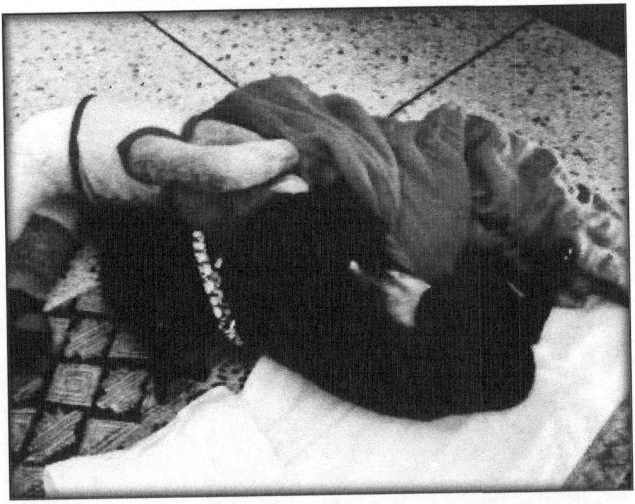

Sultan, sleeping with his toy

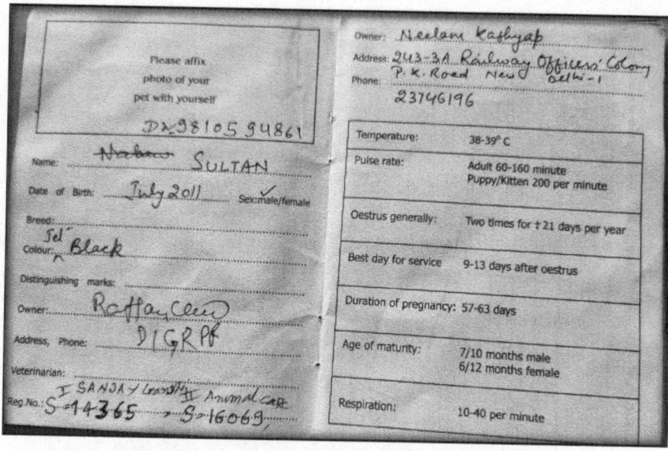

Please affix photo of your pet with yourself

DL 9810594861

Name: ~~Nabaw~~ SULTAN

Date of Birth: July 2011 Sex: male/female ✓

Breed:

Colour: Jet Black

Distinguishing marks:

Owner:

Address, Phone: DIGRPf

Veterinarian: I SANJAY Gandhi II Animal Care

Reg.No.: S-14365 S-16069

Owner: Neelam Kashyap

Address: 243-3A Railway Officers' Colony P.K. Road New Delhi-1

Phone: 23746196

Temperature:	38-39° C
Pulse rate:	Adult 60-160 minute Puppy/Kitten 200 per minute
Oestrus generally:	Two times for ± 21 days per year
Best day for service	9-13 days after oestrus
Duration of pregnancy:	57-63 days
Age of maturity:	7/10 months male 6/12 months female
Respiration:	10-40 per minute

Sultan's, medical record of first visit to veterinary clinic near Tis Hajari Courts

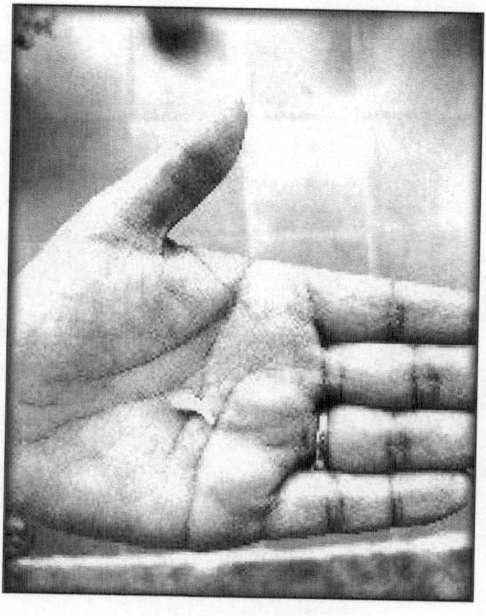

Sultan's, fallen milk teeth

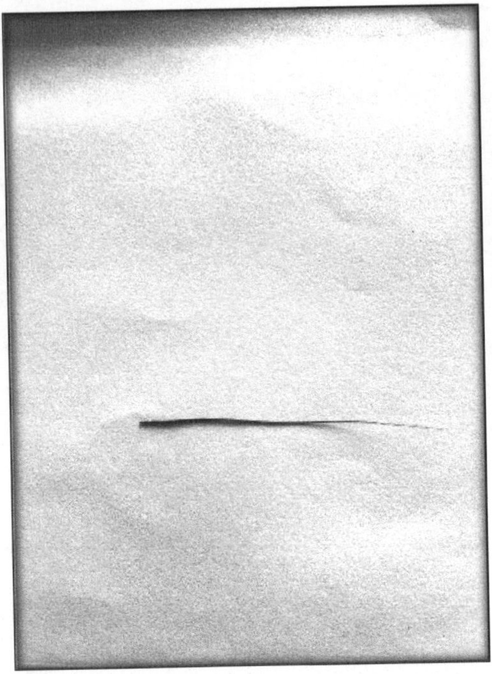

Sultan's whisker pulled by Madhav

Gabbar and Sultan

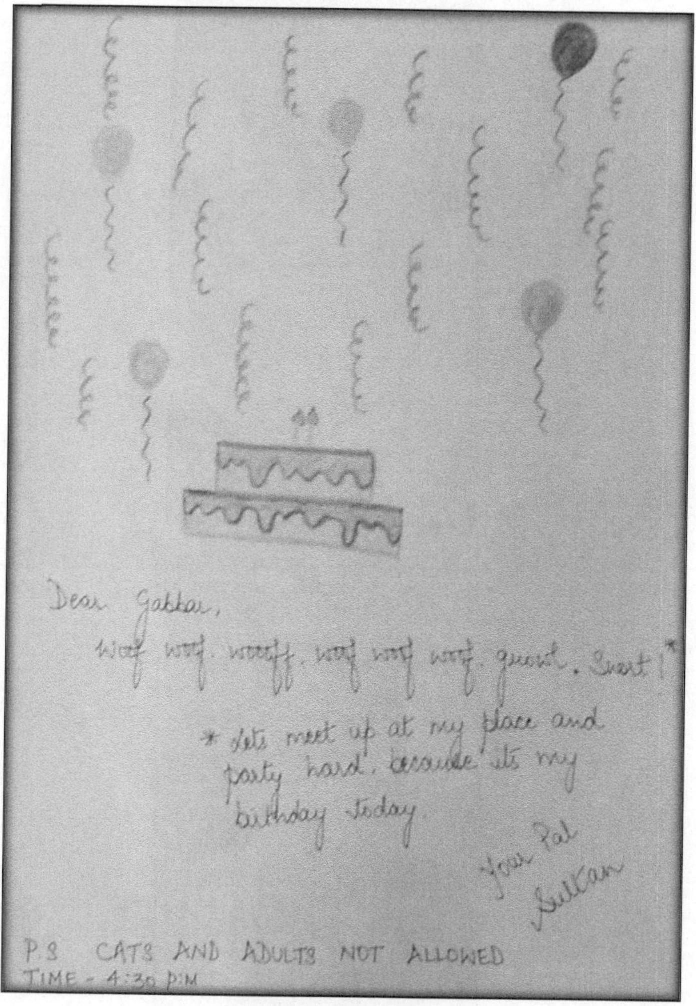

Dear Gabbar,

Woof woof. wooff. woof woof woof. growl. Snort!*

* lets meet up at my place and party hard. because its my birthday today.

Your Pal
Sultan

P.S CATS AND ADULTS NOT ALLOWED
TIME - 4:30 P.M

Sultan's birthday invite to Gabbar.

Gabbar's birthday gift sent to Sultan

Sultan wearing birthday cap

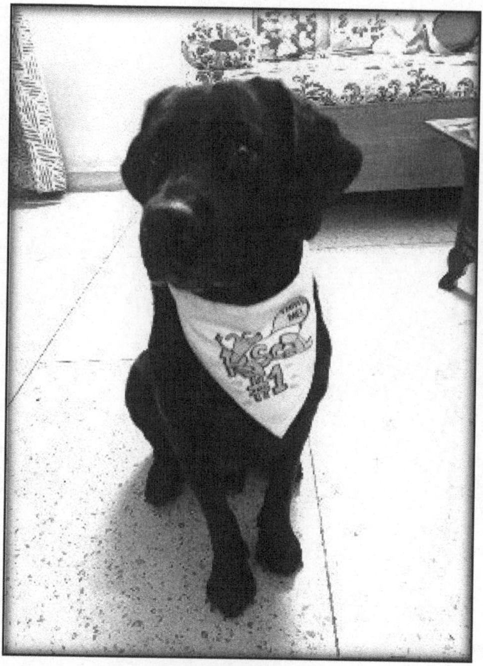

Sultan wearing a bandana

Mrs. Deepti Lalchand with Flunky

Nicky and Cherie

Sultan's balls and dog toy with moving neck

TV and its base broken by Madhav and Sultan

Mahinder

Sahab Singh Meena

Retd. SI, Dog Squad, Bhanwar Singh

Master Shifu

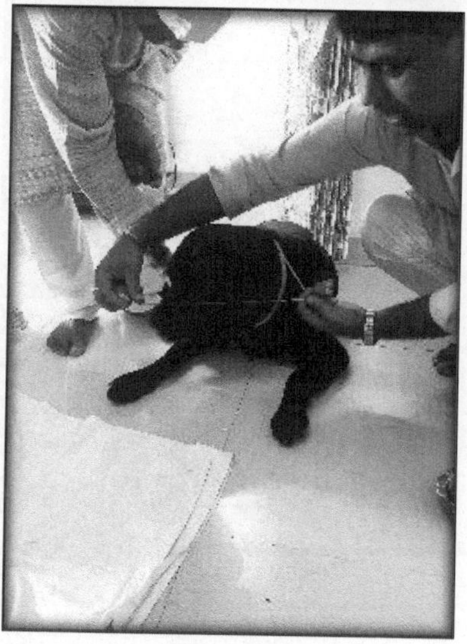

Pandit ji tying sacred thread around Sultan's neck during Puja

Sultan during boat ride in River Brahmputra, with Mom and Rajbongshi

Sultan near Pandu Port with Garima and Mom

Sultan in saloon, with Mom and Papa

Sultan with Boro in saloon

Sultan with Toffee

Sultan sitting in his kitchen garden in Guwahati

Empty packets of treats and jingle bell toy brought by Garima, for Sultan.

Brahmo

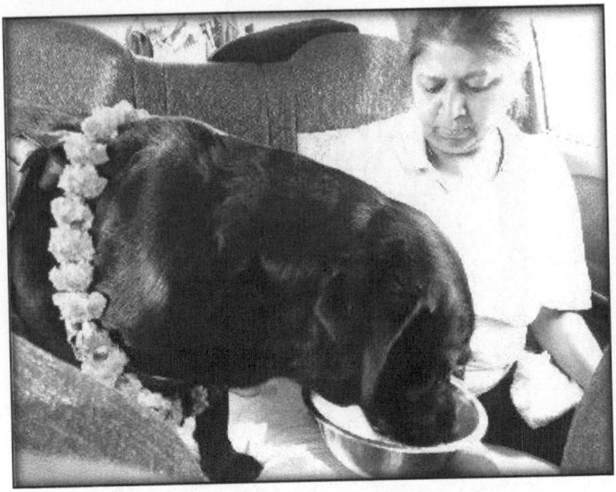

Sultan welcomed by Mom after his arrival from Guwahati

Sultan with Paswan and Guddi

Madhav holding Sultan

Kai, Sultan's friend

Rajbongshi

Satyendra

Chapter 81

A Storm in Our Lives

One morning when we entered the lift, we turned around to see that three children were already present there. The moment they saw me, they started patting my back, and I wagged my tail in response. When we had reached the ground, we started walking towards the society park and the children started playing with me. Mom was deliberately keeping me on one side of the park. When a young boy saw me, he started playing with me, taking me to the center of the lawn. Mom asked him many times not to take me to where other children were playing but he didn't listen. He opened my leash and started dragging it while running. I started chasing him, and other children joined us. We were having fun while Mom was asking me to come back but her voice was lost in the commotion.

In the meantime one old lady entered the lawn with her granddaughter. The moment the lady saw me she started shouting at me blindly. She started yelling, "Who has allowed this dog here? It is dangerous for our children, our children can get infections from it. Whose dog is this?" Mom tried to talk to her but she just didn't listen. She was yelling at the top of her voice, calling the guard to the park and asking him to shoo me away. The guard told Mom that dogs were not allowed on the lawn. In the meantime, Mom got a phone call. While she was on the phone, I could tell she was clarifying her stand to somebody.

After a few minutes we went back to our flat. Papa was sitting in the study room as usual. Mom went to him and tried to narrate the incident to him but before she could start, Papa said that he already knew what had happened on the lawn. He said, "I know what had happened in the lawn. I have already gotten a phone call from the previous president of the Residents Welfare Association (RWA) of our society. That woman spoke to him and told him everything."

He continued, "What was the need to take Sultan to the part of the society that is meant for children?" When Mom heard this, she tried to justify her stand. Papa was quite convinced but he said, "Very soon we are going to have our RWA's meeting and I am sure that this issue will be raised by the lady. She was also insisting that dogs should be banned from the lifts and public areas. I am sure all the anti-animal residents will support her. I, too, have to make my arguments ready."

It was clear that there was a problem awaiting us. I was sure that all the pet dogs were soon going to face a storm. Would all the dogs have to take stairs from now on? I started thinking about my friend Kai, my only friend in the society. Whenever we met each other we used to lick each other out of affection. I was on the sixth floor, so going down the stairs was still bearable… but what about Kai? How would he manage to go up and down the stairs every time from the tenth floor?

After this incident, I started having nightmares. Sometimes I would see myself taking the stairs up to my floor, puffing and panting, out of breath. Sometimes I would see all the dogs using the stairs, all at once. I used to shudder at the very thought. I spent the next few days in great suspense, thinking that our future depended on the verdict of the RWA. The days seemed to be passing very slowly, and the wait was becoming unbearable.

We were given an interim relief that we could use the lift at least up until the final verdict of the RWA, but what after that?

Chapter 82

The Happy Ending

After an unbearable wait, the day finally came. The RWA meeting was to be held soon. When Papa told us about it, my heart started throbbing. I had been bouncing between great tension and suspense all these days. Finally, the day had arrived and Papa got ready for the meeting. Before leaving, he told us not to worry and that everything would be alright.

Unfortunately, his words didn't give me any solace. Mom looked tense too. Kai and his Mom came to our house that day, and Mom started discussing the matter with them. Aunty Ruby said to Mom, "What kind of an insensitive society is this? How can they be so dictatorial and give such an order? Kai goes out five times a day, will he go up and down the stairs five times from the tenth floor?"

She looked at Mom with a determined expression.

"Sunny told me about the Animal Welfare Board of India. According to its rules, pets can't be denied the right to use lifts. If our RWA makes the wrong decision, we will approach the AWBI."

Mom replied, "That's fine, Ruby. That will be our last resort. We have another platform: PETA. We can approach them, too, but my point is that neither of these organisations will give their decision on the same day. It will take at least fifteen days, until then our dogs will take the stairs. Are we ready for that?"

Aunt Ruby looked convinced and said, "Let's hope your husband comes home with good news."

Both of them kept talking about Kai and I and the problems we were going to face. After some time, the doorbell rang. Mom hurriedly got up and opened the door to see it was Papa! The moment he entered, Mom and Aunty Ruby started peppering him with questions. He patiently told them not to worry and everything would be fine for the pets in the colony. Mom and Aunt Ruby both heaved a sigh of relief after hearing him say that. Kai and I started licking each other out of excitement. In the meantime, Papa went to change clothes. When he came back to the living room, he asked for a glass of water as he sat down at the dining table. Mom quickly brought water for him, and when he was through, he started narrating everything.

"A lot happened. More than I had anticipated. The regular issues were discussed first, then the issue of dogs arose. The entire Association became divided into a pro-dog and an anti-dog lobby. The anti-dog lobby was of the opinion that entry of dogs should be banned in the lifts and parks altogether. They even went to the extent of saying that no dogs should be allowed to live in our society and that no owner should rent his flat to a dog-owning family because dogs are dirty! I couldn't believe anyone could hate dogs so much."

Mom asked him about the reaction of the pro-dog lobby and Papa continued.

"They asked how they could afford to keep their flat vacant in wait for such tenants. Moreover, many owners have dogs too. Does the Association want them to sell off their flats because they have dogs? The owners were of the opinion that they would have to bring the matter to the notice of the Animals Welfare Board of India, which clearly says that dogs can not be prohibited in the lifts and in common areas when they are taken for a walk." Papa continued, "I didn't need to defend Sultan, the pro-dog lobby itself solved the matter and the anti-dog lobby had to keep quiet."

After listening to him, Mom and Aunt Ruby hugged each other and us out of joy. Aunty Ruby said to Papa, "You've given us happy news today. All the days spent waiting for this verdict were full of tension. Finally, I feel relieved! I want to share this news with my family, so I would like to take your leave." She took Kai and left with a look of satisfaction on her face.

Papa's words had given me relief too. My heart started jumping with joy. I became grateful to the RWA for solving the problems being faced by pet dogs for good. Mom gave me another hug and thanked Papa.

"There are many people who don't like pets and animals", Mom said to Papa. "No one can make them change their opinion and they shouldn't. Everyone has the right to think what they think... but at the same time, it just doesn't sit right with me that someone should hate animals quite so much. I wish I could tell them that they don't have to like our pets, but they shouldn't hate them either."

Papa told her to forget about all of this.

"Our problem is solved for good. It was definitely an unwanted stress that we had to bear, but as of today we are tension-free. All's well that ends well."

The whole ordeal had ended in our favour and we would never have any issues using the lift again. In a way, the whole thing reminded me of how my life had been up until this point. There were always problems and issues that seemed overbearing and concerning. In the end, though, my family's love for me always persevered and everything always turned out fine. I got to experience so many wonderful things that all dogs deserve in their life! I couldn't wait to see what happened next, and I was ready to face it all with my loving family by my side.

I would tell it all, in the story of Sultan.